The Bible as Politics

The Rape of Dinah
and other stories

The Bible as Politics

The Rape of Dinah
and other stories

Andrew Parker

Circle Books

Winchester, UK
Washington, USA

First published by Circle Books, 2013
Circle Books is an imprint of John Hunt Publishing Ltd., Laurel House, Station Approach,
Alresford, Hants, SO24 9JH, UK
office1@jhpbooks.net
www.johnhuntpublishing.com
www.circle-books.com

For distributor details and how to order please visit the 'Ordering' section on our website.

Text copyright: Andrew Parker 2013

ISBN: 978 1 78099 249 5

A CIP catalogue record for this book is available from the British Library.

Design: Stuart Davies

Printed and bound by CPI Group (UK) Ltd, Croydon, CR0 4YY

We operate a distinctive and ethical publishing philosophy in all
areas of our business, from our global network of authors to
production and worldwide distribution.

CONTENTS

Andrew Parker

Studied Divinity at New College, Edinburgh in the mid sixties and was ordained as the assistant minister in Dunfermline Abbey. Finding himself hooked on the Bible's extraordinary political insights but coming to the conclusion that he had no interest whatsoever in religion, he joined the French Protestant Industrial Mission, earning his living as an unskilled manual worker. He was expelled from France in 1973 for 'political activities unbecoming in a foreigner' and settled in Castlemilk, Glasgow working first as a garage mechanic and then as a porter in a psychiatric hospital.

Andrew started using cartoons to communicate (since his workmates would not read anything else) and share his ideas on the Bible. He came to realise he did not know enough about the Bible to communicate it properly and so decided to do his own research moving at the same time to the east end of London.

Having finally worked things out to his own satisfaction and having retired as Deputy Head Porter at St Pancras Hospital, Andrew has returned to the job of expounding the Bible.

He has written several books:

Painfully Clear: The Parables of Jesus (Sheffield Academic Press 1996)
Searing Light: Parables for Preachers
Light Denied: A Challenge to Scholars
God of the Marginals: The Ideology Demonstrated by Jesus

the last three of which can be accessed on his website www.bibleincartoons.co.uk

Andrew is also presently working on a four-volume cartoon work on the Bible, the first two volumes of which are published on Blurb Books and can also be downloaded from his website.

This book has been from start to finish a joint venture with Julie Mansfield and John Rowe. The basic ideas are mine. Their contribution has been to help in making it all understandable, which has not always been easy for the Bible says very uncomfortable things.

The texts dealt with in this book were not carefully selected as the *best* stories to illustrate my thesis that there is a revolutionary Hebrew/Marginal ideology lying at the heart of the Bible for I believe this thesis can equally well be illustrated using almost any selection of stories from the Bible. The stories were selected simply with an eye to covering as much of the ground as possible so as to gain a reasonably overall picture.

Introduction

Is the Bible a Political or Religious Work?

There are a number of stories in the Bible, such as The Rape of Dinah, which cause preachers (and others) all sorts of problems. They would rather such distasteful stories did not exist. I find this alarming for if you are unable to appreciate the significance of a crucial story such as The Rape of Dinah I fail to see how you can begin to understand the Bible at all. That may sound a big claim ... and it is ... but I am hoping that if you allow me a little of your time I will be able to demonstrate that this and other Bible stories make perfect if disturbing sense without requiring you to suspend your God-given powers of logic and common-sense. You will then begin to see that the Bible's unique marginal insight and the vision of its Hebrew heroes are more compelling now than they ever were.

However, we must not run before we can walk. There are certain things we need to consider. To begin with we have to think about what kind of book the Bible is. This may require you to re-examine your current understanding for my contention is that the Bible is not essentially a religious book. Unsurprisingly, people are flummoxed when I say the Bible is talking more about politics (ordinary human relationships) than religion (however we define it. Please see below.). Even when I point out that the texts from the ancient Near East which most resemble those found in the Bible demonstrate little interest in religion while being intensely political they still don't get it, so firmly is it established in their heads that the Bible is a religious book.

Some people will reply that you can't compare the Bible with other ancient texts because the Bible alone comes as a direct revelation from God. This might have some weight as an argument could it be shown that the Bible is culturally idiosyncratic, as a Confucian document would be if it suddenly appeared out of the blue in the ancient Near East. For if privileged information had been revealed by God then it would have been absolutely necessary to deal with this in a completely new way by telling stories of a completely different kind; stories which took into account this amazing paradigm shift. But this did not happen. The Israelites told exactly the same kind of mythical stories as other people did ... though in such a manner *as to give a completely different understanding of the world.* It is painfully evident therefore that the Bible shares a common religio-mythical culture with other texts of its time and locality which means that it has to be seen as comparable with them.

Religion: A Word Full of Confusion

Part of our problem is in having no clear idea of what religion is. People take it for granted they know what religion means, yet when I ask them whether Buddhism is a religion they answer 'Yes and No' which doesn't really help! It would be good if we could all stop using the word religion and find an alternative which is more precise. However, that's clearly not on the cards. So let me try and clarify the situation by sketching out for you how I think what we speak about as religion arose in our own civilisation, which started somewhere around 5,000 years ago in the ancient Near East.

Myth: A Language for Talking Politics

It all began with people wanting to talk about the powers in the world which affected them. These were not just natural powers like the sun, wind and rain. There were also *human political forces* like enemies, the local community, the extended family, brothers and sisters not forgetting Mum and Dad. The trouble was that the ancients had little or no political vocabulary for talking about such powers so they were obliged to invent a language of their own. They did this by the simple expedient of personalising these forces. So they spoke about the sun as a god and even Mum's power could be expressed simply by referring to her personal spirit. We call this language which the ancients developed for talking about politics, the mythological superstructure.

You could say that what we have here is the beginning of religion. However, all we are talking about so far is vocabulary: words and symbols designed to represent experienced phenomena. Mythological language is found all over the ancient Near East, and, of course, in the Bible as well. But the important thing to realise is that the presence of mythological language in an ancient text does not imply the presence of religion for, as we have just said, mythological language is designed to talk about experienced powers, not imagined ones; which is to say *politics* not *religion*. We seriously confuse ourselves by talking about myth as religious language. Myth is political language, not religious language and this is crucial to understanding the Bible.

Religion 1: Myth-Talk as Superstition

What happened next was unfortunate but inevitable. Having personalised these natural forces (sun, wind, river etc) in order to talk about them, it was now a short step to taking this person-alisation literally and to seeing these described forces as influence-able through prayer and offerings. Here we find ourselves dealing with something more than just vocabulary and representation. Here we have superstition which, for many, is just another word for religion[1]. Let's call this Religion 1: the basic phenomenon traceable wherever human language has been recorded.

There are, however, two other phenomena commonly spoken about as religion. These both stem from the Bible and they are found in no other ancient writings. To appreciate what they are we must first understand the Bible properly as an ideological endeavour[2].

Since there had been no bourgeois or proletarian revolutions in the ancient world, all the civilisations in the ancient Near East, without exception, were ideologically conservative[3] and quite naturally their mythologies reflect this basic fact. However, uniquely as far as we know, the Bible at its heart encapsulates a *revolutionary* endeavour of some description. We have to be a little careful with this word because we tend to think of revolutions as coercive and class-based. This is not true of the revolution of which the Bible speaks for here we are dealing with a marginal 'revolution' and marginals have no coercive potential since they do not constitute a class within society. Marginals can come from any and every section of society. For what marks them out is not their social origins but the simple fact that they have *failed*, whether this be due to their own fault or fate it really does not matter. Throughout the whole of the second millennium BCE civilisation officials all over the ancient Near East referred to such people as 'Apiru', 'Abiru' or Hebrews and from what they wrote it is clear they considered such people not as members of society but as sub-human dogs[4].

At its heart the Bible describes the Hebrew ideological struggle. Finding themselves dustbinned and so outside civilisation altogether, these marginals saw the world fundamentally differently from the ruling conservative elites who ran the existing establishments. Their standpoint was that no-one should be allowed to fall out of society's net and that anyone in danger of doing so had a legitimate call on his/her fellow human-beings. As they put it, *people should love their neighbour as they loved themselves* (Leviticus 19.18).

These Hebrews formed the leadership of a new community called Israel which established itself in the early iron-age in the central highlands of Palestine. *And the Bible is the story of Israel's attempt to demonstrate this standpoint ... something which, much later, the disciples saw Jesus himself as fulfilling.*

All the anti-*status quo* texts in the Bible are written from this marginal Hebrew perspective. This means that the god Yahweh, around whom these texts are written, has to be seen as the god of the marginals or, according to the common myth-linguistics of the time, as the god representing the marginals' political power and aspirations. (I should perhaps make it plain that every community in the ancient Near East had its own god to represent it; as for example, Kemosh who represented the Moabites. When it came to empire civilisations like the Sumerians, the gods representing different sections of society were gathered together in a pantheon run by a group of ruling gods; as for example Enlil who, for the Mesopotamians, represented the military elite and Enki who represented the administrative elite.)

Religion 2: The Metacosmic God as a Hope Against Hope

So far so good. Now we come to the interesting bit. According to the common myth-linguistics of the ancient world, if Yahweh represented the political power of the marginals he could only be the weakest and most miserable of all the gods. For the Hebrew marginals this contradicted their experience. It was true the surrounding conservative ideologies had all the fire-power; however, the way they operated was as manufacturers of spiritual[5] and physical death. Conversely, though he possessed no fire-power at all, Yahweh operated as the source of all life and humanity. So how were they to express this experience? The answer is mind-blowing. They suggested that whilst all the conservative gods, in being dependant on and part of the universe, were cosmic Yahweh, for his part, was not.

Since we do not have a word to express this idea I have coined one, calling Yahweh the metacosmic god. But how did the biblical writers manage? Well, just as the conservative civilisations described their cosmic gods as having needs and appetites which humans could use to gain influence over them, the

Hebrews described their god as having no such needs and appetites being completely above such things which, as they saw it, were all part and parcel of what Yahweh had created rather than being aspects of himself. This was formalised much later by describing Yahweh as the god who created the universe *out of nothing*, though such a description is not found in the Bible itself[6].

Now, there is no denying that what I call the metacosmic god, namely this god who has no needs or appetites which the cosmos can satisfy, is a religious idea of some description making the belief in such a god a religious phenomenon. So let's call it Religion 2. Properly understood, this metacosmic god idea is not so much a firmly held religious belief as a gesture of ideological defiance. Paul the apostle described it as a hope against hope (Romans 4.18) and I think that puts it rather well. I see it myself as a bet which the marginals made against civilisation, where the stake consisted of their life and everything. That, it seems to me, is the sort of religion which the revolutionary biblical writers, and Jesus himself, spoke about and it has nothing to do with superstition or even with the final kind of religion we must now discuss which too is found in the Bible and nowhere else ... but only in what I see as its revisionist texts.

Religion 3: The God of the Biblical Revisionists

It would be grand if we could simply leave it at that. However, the unfortunate truth is that there were those within the leadership of the community who sought to change this marginal revolutionary programme by softening and obscuring the revolutionary objective which they rightly saw was inimical to their own interests as leaders. I call these people 'revisionists' because they sought to back-track by reverting to the civilisation norm of a conservative, authoritarian deity. Fortunately, they did this not by rewriting the old revolutionary stories but simply by presenting them in such a way that people read them in a non-revolutionary, conservative fashion. This means that it is still possible to read the stories as they were originally intended to be read. However, it takes an effort and you have to know what is going on.

In the main, the problem faced by the revisionists was how to hide or, better still, get rid of the god of the marginals altogether while maintaining those characteristics pertaining to him which could be made to fit with the aspirations and worldview of Israel's increasingly conservative leadership. What this amounted to was replacing the god of the marginals, who as such was also the metacosmic Lord of the Universe, with a new metacosmic yet conservative god who demanded nothing but obedience to the commands issued in his name by his priests. This change essentially meant getting rid of *an ideological* god who represented the marginals' clear-sighted and easily checkable way of seeing things and replacing him with *a religious* god who represented the blinkered vision of those in authority, whose commands had to be obeyed blindly and without question simply because he was *a religious* god. Though this change was clearly deliberate it does not necessarily follow that it took place brutally and instantaneously. However, the final consequence was the development of the idea of God as the all powerful interfering conservative deity. Unfortunately this is the idea that automatically springs into many people's minds when the word God is used today regardless of whether they believe in such a God or not. Richard Dawkins reckons that belief in this interfering God amounts to superstitious nonsense and I have to say I think that in this, if in little else concerning the Bible, he is quite right.

I

The Creation Myth (Genesis 1)

The Revisionist Editor's Authoritarian Stamp.

The Youngest Myth in the Bible

Since it is found on page 1, you might legitimately think the story of creation is the oldest myth in the Bible. In fact, it is almost certainly the youngest. During most of the twentieth century the general consensus was that it was written by a priestly writer in the post-exilic period (which is to say, after the Persian emperor Cyrus had issued his decree that the exiles who had formerly been carted off to Babylon should be allowed to return home.) Recently, however, a number of scholars have argued that *all* the texts in Genesis should be dated as post-exilic which makes life difficult. That said, I still believe there are over-riding reasons why this myth, which is stylistically quite unlike the others, should be understood as a late offering.

A Remarkable Difference

As we will shortly see, there is clear evidence to suggest that Genesis 1 is a re-write of the much older Mesopotamian creation myths[7]. That said, it is hard to ignore how different it is from them. The Mesopotamian creation myths are based on the understanding that the gods carved out the universe from an existing primeval chaos in order to create a pleasant environment for them to live in given their needs. This means the work was done without regard for the interests of *mortal* creatures including mankind. When you think about it, having due regard for the ancients' mythical way of expressing themselves, this is pretty much the way in which we scientifically view things today, for we also see the universe as the creation of natural, cosmic forces which operate in a manner that betrays not the slightest regard for human creatures like us. So you could say that what the Mesopotamian writers present is simply the natural way of seeing things. Genesis 1, on the contrary, does not envisage the universe as being created by a multitude of natural forces. Rather it states that everything, including the natural cosmic forces themselves, was created by a single power that was itself totally unlike anything it created since it alone betrays no dependence in the form of desires or needs. Further to this, Genesis 1 describes this 'metacosmic' power as bestowing on mankind authority in order to provide all living creatures with proper rule. In conclusion, therefore, it would seem that whereas the Mesopotamians present the natural way of looking at the universe, Genesis 1 provides an unnatural or religious perspective which sees the universe as being created by a power that from the very start had mankind in mind.

An Equally Remarkable Similarity

So much for this very surprising difference between the general perspectives offered by Genesis 1 and the Mesopotamian creation myths. What about their equally surprising similarity? Given the remarkable difference we have just noted you might expect Genesis 1 to exhibit a completely different *political* perspective or ideology from that found in the Mesopotamian myths. However, as we shall see, the surprising thing is that ideologically the texts are virtually indistinguishable.

The Imago Dei

The Mesopotamian myths tell us that the gods were so pissed off with the irksome toil involved in providing themselves with food, drink and housing that they went on strike, surrounding the palace where the ruling gods were ensconced and making a great commotion. To save the situation, Enki the priestly administrators' god, decided to fabricate a slave creature to do the gods' work for them. Thus Man was created. However, in order

9

to render Man capable of doing the gods' work it was necessary to endow him with some of the gods' own wisdom. For this reason one of the gods was slain and his blood mixed with the clay which was to be used in making Man. In this way the process of fabrication ensured that Man became endowed with wisdom and personality, the process itself being summed up in the phrase that 'Man was made in the image of the gods'. Fully equipped Man was then given the priestly role of building temples for the gods and of providing the necessary sacrifices. This was the Mesopotamian writers' way of saying that as they saw things, Man's role in the universe was to be the administrator of creation. Using our own terms you could say that they saw the universe as being like a farm; the gods being the owners and the humans the farm managers whose job it was to see that the farm remained productive for the owners' benefit. Given this picture it is not difficult to see that the writers of the Mesopotamian myths operated with a *status quo*, conservative ideology or worldview which enabled them to justify their own authoritarian position in society on the grounds of their superior wisdom and administrative skills. Furthermore, it is not difficult to work out that the lynch-pin holding this authoritarian, conservative ideology together was the idea that man was made in the image of the gods. As you can see the writer of Genesis 1 stole this wretched construct from the Mesopotamians, lock stock and barrel:

Then God said, 'Let us make man in our image, in our likeness, and let them rule over the fish of the sea and the birds of the air, over the livestock, over all the earth, and over all the creatures that move along the ground.' So God created man in his own image, in the image of God he created him; male and female he created them. God blessed them and said to them, 'Be fruitful and increase in number; fill the earth and subdue it. Rule over the fish of the sea and the birds of the air

and over every living creature that moves on the ground.'
(Genesis 1:26-28)

Furthermore, because he inserted this passage so prominently at
the beginning of everything it has become necessary for people
who read the Bible to try and make something good out of it. My
objective, however, is to try to get readers to see it for what it is;
namely a stinking bit of second hand, conservative authoritari-
anism, and to think about what the writer was doing in sticking
it there.

Conservative Politics but where has the Metacosmic Idea Come From?

It's true that, in contrast to the reasoning in the Mesopotamian
myths, there is not the slightest hint in this Bible passage that
man's job is to make the creation fruitful for the benefit of God.
Saying that would have indicated that God had needs which,
given his metacosmic nature, would have been blasphemy.
Consequently, the whole thing is left rather unsatisfactorily open
and unresolved in a way which simply suggests that it should
somehow be obvious that human society *has* to be organised in
an authoritarian manner. I think the Mesopotamian writers
would have found this reasoning weak. However, they would
certainly have approved of Genesis 1's main ideological lines
since they were the ones who had invented them.

So it's not difficult to see where all of this right-wing *ideology*
in Genesis 1 has come from. It is, however, more difficult to
explain whence came this extraordinary *religious* idea of the
metacosmic god who has no needs or desires for it was certainly
not the Mesopotamians who invented it … or any other civilisation that we know of in the ancient world for that matter.
Religious people sometimes try to explain its appearance by
saying that it came by way of revelation which, in being magical,
is of course no explanation at all. In the introduction I have

already provided you with my own account of how this extraordinary idea developed out of a marginal hope-against-hope and I think you will agree that such an explanation demands no fairytale suspension of disbelief.

Adam and Eve and The Garden of Eden (Genesis 2-3)

The Marginal Revolutionary Vision of a World Without Status

Another Story Pinched from the Mesopotamians

This text too is clearly based on a pre-existing Mesopotamian myth: the story of Adapa. Adapa and Adam both mean Man. Though this similarity is striking a much more important similarity lies in the fact that both stories are constructed along the same unusual lines. Both are concerned with the question of Man's essential nature given that, though he possesses certain qualities, like mortality, which align him with all the other animals, he also possesses other qualities, like wisdom, or call it what you will, which mark him off as 'godly'. And let me point out that this is not a religious question as you might be thinking. It is simply a mythological way of discussing a very down-to-earth matter which confronts us all. For manifestly there are important ways in which we are superior to the other animals but *what are the implications of this superiority as regards our behaviour?*

In the Adapa Story Man is in charge ... but he has to be careful

In the specific terms of the Adapa myth, Man is said to share his mortality with the other animals; however, unlike them he has been endowed with personality and wisdom, meaning by this administrative nous. According to the story this has been done so that he may perform his allotted task of *managing the creation* for the gods and it gives him *status* and *authority* over the rest of creation, including all the other animals. Man therefore can use this god-given authority as he sees fit so long as he is careful not to step on any godly toes. Once again, if you make due allowance for their mythological expression, it seems to me that the Mesopotamian scribes are here simply describing the situation as we ourselves largely see it. For isn't it true we too are aware that the trait which distinguishes us from the other animals gives us a power which we are at liberty to use as we see fit, just so long as we are careful not to disrupt any of the natural processes governing the universe, thereby inadvertently bringing catastrophe on our heads? Indeed, isn't this precisely what the genetically-modified-foods debate is all about? No-one is concerned to argue that we shouldn't use our knowledge to make nature more productive. What bothers people is that we don't truly know what will be the consequences of our actions and thus we risk inadvertently doing something very stupid and costly to ourselves. The only possible caveat we would make is that perhaps the Mesopotamian writers move a bit too easily from saying that Man has a power other creatures don't have (which is obvious) to saying that therefore Man has authority to do what he sees fit, which I suspect some people, though probably not many, might be wary of today.

What's the Score in the Adam Story?

What then has the Garden of Eden story to say about all this? Since it is quite involved let's look at it in stages:

Is Genesis 2-3 an Authoritarian Text?

First, we need to think about the essential difference between Genesis 1 and Genesis 2-3. Have you ever noticed how in Genesis 2-3 *the creation starts all over again* but this time in a different order and no word at all about Man being made in God's image? This should start some alarm bells ringing that Genesis 1 and Genesis 2-3 have different authors. Well, that's no big deal of itself. What is the big deal in my book is that these two Genesis stories have been written from opposite ideological perspectives. You will remember that Genesis 1 is written from a conservative viewpoint which the writer uses to justify Man's authority over all living creatures. Compare this with Genesis 2-3 which says nothing openly on the subject of man's status or authority over the other animals. Consequently, for those who find it necessary to make the stories square with one another, this matter of authority has either to be assumed in Genesis 2-3 or else some way has to be found of reading it between the lines. Three ways have been suggested for doing this:

1. It is often argued that in being created first, Man is presumed to have authority. The problem here is that in Genesis 1, where there is no doubt that Man has authority, he is created last not first.

2. It is often argued that, in designating Adam as the gardener, the myth endows humans with status, for in the ancient Near East the title of gardener is sometimes used of the King. However, Genesis 2-3 does not say that Yahweh designates Adam as his gardener or that Adam is given the title gardener. In fact, the word gardener never appears in the text. Furthermore there is no suggestion that Yahweh wants Adam to look after the garden for him, nor is there any evidence that Yahweh considers the garden as a property he wishes to exploit. This whole scenario of Adam being the gardener in Eden is a fabrication and demonstrates how *we* think (and how the writer of Genesis 1 thought) and not how the writer of Genesis 2-3 thought.

3. It is often argued that Yahweh confers kingly status on Adam by getting him to give the animals their names. We do know of a number of occasions when kings in the ancient Near East emphasised the subordinate state of certain key officials by giving them new names. The problem with this argument is that there is no evidence that name-giving in the

ancient Near East was taken as a sign of a person's hierarchical status so no-one reading the Garden of Eden story would have made such a deduction, especially given the fact that Adam was the only animal capable of speech and so of giving names.

Genesis 2-3 is Not an Authoritarian Text

In fact, this whole business of trying to find an authoritarian outlook in the text by reading between the lines is misplaced. Had the writer wished to say that Adam had hierarchical or, more correctly, centrarchical[8] status he would have made it perfectly clear, just as both the Mesopotamian scribes and the writer of Genesis 1 did. He would not have left people to deduce such a crucial matter from secondary features in his story. Genesis 2-3 recounts that having created Adam, Yahweh supplies him with a garden to live in just as people supply a horse they have bought with a field. The object of the exercise is not to give Adam a managerial position so that he can organise the exploitation of the property for his boss. Rather it is to provide Adam with an environment so that he can live in freedom feeding himself, the whole question of status being *immaterial.*

Genesis 2-3 Rejects Authoritarianism

The fact that Genesis 2-3 specifically rejects the Mesopotamian authoritarian line is emphasised by the way it describes the crucial trait which distinguishes Man from the animals. The Mesopotamian text, for its part, speaks about this trait as wisdom, meaning 'administrative nous' which is clearly an authoritarian characteristic. However, Genesis 2 calls the trait 'the knowledge of good and evil'. Now, there is a difficulty here, for the fact is that these ancient writers had no term for an awareness; a psychological state for which no word had as yet been coined. They could only talk about consciousness by speaking about it as a knowledge, which is not quite the same thing. This creates a major problem for us because this biblical text is all about human awareness: our consciousness of our sexuality, our consciousness of our mortality and our consciousness of our capacity to sin. This means that we have to concentrate hard on what the writer is trying to say so as not to read things into the texts which are not there. For example, here you might find yourself reading this 'knowledge of good and evil' as something a person can acquire and so gain status, just as in the case of administrative wisdom. However, this would be to seriously misunderstand what the writer is trying to express, which is that knowledge of good and evil is an awareness which arrives gratuitously in a flash, as when eating a fruit, taking the recipient by surprise just as all awarenesses do.

Genesis 2-3 is a Marginal Text

OK, so what does this 'good and evil' awareness consist of? Well, it involves a consciousness of right and wrong. This means that for the writer of Genesis 2-3 what distinguishes Man from the other animals is wisdom understood as *moral awareness*, not as *administrative nous*. Now the interesting thing is that though moral awareness is certainly ideologically coloured, changing as it does from one community to another, the awareness itself cannot be ideological for it exists *universally* amongst adult humans while being *universally absent* in the other species. Consequently, in actively disagreeing with the Mesopotamian scribes, who argued that Man's difference from the other animals lies in the fact that he has a unique characteristic which gives him status (i.e. marks him out as centrarchically superior) one has to suppose that the writer of Genesis 2-3 was working with a contrary, non-authoritarian ideology of some sort. The conclusion, therefore, would seem inescapable: Genesis 2-3 must have been deliberately written from a non-authoritarian, Hebrew or as we would say 'marginal' stance. I think most people today would say that the writer of Genesis 2-3 saw Man's situation more truthfully than the Mesopotamian scribes and the writer of Genesis 1, which suggests to me that his clarity of vision resulted from his non-authoritarian, marginal outlook. But let's not be too hasty. Let's first verify whether he did indeed have a non-authoritarian ideology, by looking more closely at his story.

A Dangerous Tree Designed to test Obedience?

The story starts with Yahweh creating Adam. This job completed, he plants a garden for Adam to live in. He then instructs Adam to feed himself by growing crops and gathering fruit. However, he makes it unmistakably clear (by the process of issuing a command) that there is one tree in the garden, the tree of the knowledge of good and evil, the fruit of which Adam must not eat because it means death. This raises the question of the significance of this tree. Why does Yahweh not want the humans to eat its fruit and why does he include such a dangerous object in the environment he provides for this new creature? Traditionally, these kinds of questions have not been put to the text, which (slavishly following Genesis 1) is seen as making a very simple religious point about the necessity of blindly obeying God. Traditionally it is said you do not ask an authoritarian figure such as God why he issues his commands, for that is his business. Others have noted the serpent's allegation that God only issued his command because he did not want to be faced with rivals. However, it has been easy for those slavishly following Genesis 1 to dismiss such an allegation as ridiculous, given the fact that Yahweh is the untouchable Lord of the Universe. Sidelining all of these questions, traditionalists have insisted on seeing this tree as having being placed in the garden simply to raise the question of obedience. For if God had never ordered Adam and Eve to do something or, alternatively, not to do something the question of obedience or disobedience would never have arisen. But why should this *particular* tree have been chosen to measure Adam's obedience? Once again traditionalists have spurned the question.

All in all one can't help feeling that this authoritarian reading creates nothing but problems. Worse still, it imposes on the story a general form, namely punishment for disobedience, which can only be qualified as monumentally banal. I have to say that if this authoritarian reading is the correct one then I know of no other authoritarian text from the ancient Near East that compares with it in being so third rate.

Or a Tree that Affords a Dangerous Awareness?

OK. So how does the story read if we see it as a non-authoritarian marginal text? Well, everything turns on how this crucial sentence is understood:

> And the LORD God commanded the man, 'You are free to eat from any tree in the garden; but you must not eat from the tree of the knowledge of good and evil, for when you eat of it you will surely die.'(Genesis 2:16-17)

There is an ambiguity here to do with the phrase 'you will die' since it can mean three quite different things. First it can indicate that the fruit is poisonous. We can exclude this because Adam and Eve don't fall sick and die. The second possibility is that Yahweh will punish with death anyone who dares to eat the fruit. This is the way in which the phrase is traditionally understood even though the threat, if it was a threat, is never carried out. There is, however, a third way of understanding the phrase which is that *people who eat the fruit will become aware of their mortality*. This reading takes into account ancient man's difficulty in talking about awarenesses. Because of a lack of psychological vocabulary it was intrinsically difficult to make it plain that eating the fruit would bring death into people's lives by suddenly making them aware of their mortality. So the simplest thing to do was to say that eating the fruit would bring death, leaving it up to people's good sense to understand what was being said.

So, which of these possibilities is right? Two things convince me the third reading must be the correct one. First, since the whole story is about the arrival of *consciousness* surely the writer must be talking about the arrival of the *consciousness* of death here? Second, Yahweh does not punish Adam and Eve with death. What is more, no explanation is given to account for this, which most certainly would have been the case had punishment been an issue. That said, I would like to point out that in the story the serpent, who is clearly described as being 'wise' after the manner of the Mesopotamian scribes, wickedly plays on this ambiguity when he informs Eve that eating the fruit will not cause her to die. In saying this he is being both truthful and untruthful, as he with his administrative cunning well knows. For though the fruit is not poisonous and though Yahweh is not going to punish Adam and Eve with death since manifestly he is not the authoritarian fool tradition has inexplicably taken him to be, the fact is that eating the fruit is going to bring death into their lives because that, as we all know, *is precisely what consciousness does.*

Man Crosses God's Will but Yahweh is No Crass Authoritarian

Given that Yahweh is not threatening punishment, but rather talking about the disastrous negative effects consciousness will bring, how are we to explain the fact that he issues a command rather than a warning? Does this not strongly suggest that eating the fruit amounts to crossing his will? The answer is that, yes, of course it does! However, the fact that Yahweh is certainly described as making his will plain by issuing a command should not of itself be seen as portraying him as an authoritarian tyrant: someone who has nothing but 'obedience or else!' in mind. Because we are civilisation-folk we see the giving of commands and hierarchy as going together. This means that, to our minds, disobeying a command and punishment also go together, whether or not the authority in question chooses to carry out the punishment. But, for marginals with their unclouded vision, this would simply not have been the case. For them, true authority was not authoritarian and hierarchy was a sign of weakness, not, as we with our mindless civilisational ideas so ludicrously suppose, of strength (see Matthew 7:29). Indeed everything suggests that what Yahweh, as god of the marginals, had in mind was nothing other than Man's *welfare*. In issuing his command, Yahweh was simply counselling Adam *in the strongest possible terms* against taking a fateful step he would most certainly later seriously regret. Now there's a powerful insight if ever there was one, for who would not choose to live without this undesirable awareness of mortality were it possible to do so without, at the same time, being deprived of other highly desirable awarenesses?

Temptation Can be Positive as well as Negative

But why does Yahweh build this whole wretched business of temptation into his garden, you may ask? Let's think about it. We have three myths (The Adapa myth, Genesis 1 and Genesis 2-3) all of which deal with the same issue: Man's difference from the other animals. Nowadays we think we know for a fact that this difference resulted from the way in which the human species naturally developed. However, the ancients never suspected this was the case since they conceived the universe as being essentially static. Consequently all of their myths have their own, quite different, ways of *imagining* how this situation arose. The Adapa myth imagines it as resulting from the gods' decision to get someone to do their work for them. Genesis 1 sees it as resulting from God's wish to have the universe properly governed and Genesis 2-3 sees it as resulting from Man's fatal *choice* to acquire moral awareness. Since *we* know, or think we know, how this essential difference arose, the mechanism by which it came about, namely evolution, is supremely important. However, what we have to remember is that in the case of all three mythmakers, the mechanism was entirely secondary. All that was important for them was how the relationship between man and the universe (including the other animals) was envisaged. This means that asking why Yahweh put temptation in Man's way is somewhat beside the point. Since the writer of Genesis 2-3 *imagines* Man becoming different from the other animals out of *choice*, the idea of temptation is *bound* to appear in his story (the actual word never occurs) since you can't have choice without taking into account all sorts of temptation. Of course, here temptation means something rather different from what it does in the context of Genesis 1. In the light (or rather darkness!) of Genesis 1, temptation is entirely negative: a prelude to centrarchical disobedience. In Genesis 2-3, as it was originally written, temptation signifies no more than a weighing up of the pros and cons before having to go on and live with the consequences of the choice.

The Serpent as the One Who Tests Obedience

The story in Genesis 2-3 relates that the serpent was the one to put the cat amongst the pigeons by asking Eve if it was true God had told them not to eat the fruit of this particular tree. He informs her that in spite of what God has said, it is perfectly safe to eat the fruit and adds that the only reason God has forbidden it is because it will make them in some way equal with him. Once again, it's natural to ask why God put such a sly creature in the garden he created for Adam and Eve. Following the line of thought that the story is essentially about obedience, traditionalists claim the serpent's presence is explained by the need for obedience to be tested: The serpent was lying of course but even a lie can function as a test of obedience.

It is a bit too easy to get rid of the point the serpent is making by calling it a lie, for there is truth as well as falsehood in what he says. Indeed the serpent is responsible for raising the issue on which the whole traditional understanding spectacularly founders since, on learning what has happened, Yahweh does not put Adam and Eve to death. People explain this by saying God withheld punishment because he was merciful. However, this is stuff and nonsense. There is nothing in the text to justify this inference, which means that if it is true we must, once again, be dealing with a bit of third-rate writing. Furthermore, if it is the case that God withheld punishment, the natural explanation is surely not that it was out of mercy but rather that it was because he realised, rather late in the day, that the punishment he had devised was quite inappropriate. This would mean that in the story God is not just authoritarian but stupid to boot; stupid like, admittedly, a lot of authoritarian people are.

Or the Serpent as Unavoidable Right-Wing Prejudice

If we read the myth in a non-authoritarian light this problem simply disappears. The story first presents Yahweh as the god of the marginals who goes out of his way to tell Adam honestly and caringly that he should not choose to acquire consciousness since, were he able to view the whole picture, he would see the game was not worth the candle. It then brings on the serpent with all of its centrarchical cunning and shows him undermining Yahweh's work, by exploiting the ambiguity in his language, to tell Eve a small truth mixed with a big lie. He explains that the result of eating the fruit will not be instant death, which is true, but adds that Yahweh wants to avoid rivals which couldn't be further from the truth. It's a magnificent piece of writing expressing profound insight for who can deny that whatever we may do to change the world it will *never* be free of cunning right-wing whisperings: deceitful half-truths designed to trip up the unwary so as to bring the best laid schemes to nothing?

Man's Decision to Disregard What God Has Said

Seeing that the fruit looks delicious and that it offers the highly desirable prospect of gaining wisdom, (by deliberately choosing this word the mythmaker gets us to see that Eve is now beginning to adopt the serpent's own misbegotten centrarchical viewpoint) Eve eats it and persuades Adam to do likewise. The result is that their eyes are opened and they become aware of their nakedness. This embarrassment about their nakedness betrays them when they next meet God so he ends up finding out what they have done.

What is the Significance of Man's Nakedness?

The question that arises here is why did eating the fruit make Adam and Eve aware of their nakedness? You might have expected them to die, which didn't happen, but you wouldn't normally have expected them suddenly to become aware of their nakedness and so embarrassed by their state. Once again, for traditionalists this is not a valid question. They say that it was necessary for God to find out what had happened so that he might punish Adam's and Eve's disobedience ... the whole point of the story. So this nakedness business is just a convenient way for the storyteller to explain that God did find out. It could have been achieved in some other way but since sin is very often envisaged as mixed up with sex, sexual awareness and embarrassment was as good a mechanism as any.

Sex as a Political Marker

But this will not do. Sex plays a major role in these early stories since it is used as a representation, which is to say, *as a way of talking politics*: the central issue. Thus, for example in the story of the sons of Noah, when Ham is accused of seeing his father's nakedness, not something one might immediately think was especially significant, it soon becomes clear that this is simply the writer's way of saying that the descendants of Ham (namely

Israel's arch-enemies the Egyptians and the Canaanites) ideolog-ically stank. However, in this story about Adam and Eve we are not talking about a particular sexual misdemeanour but rather about *a general sexual awareness*. This story tells us that when consciousness arrives in us humans it comes as a package. This is verifiably true. You can't have moral awareness just by itself since along with moral awareness comes sexual embarrassment as well as an awareness of death, both of which people could well do without. But that is not all because, as I have said, sexual awareness in this story stands for *ideological awareness*. What the story tells us therefore is that in becoming generally conscious we become at the same time acutely aware that our natural desire to have our own way is irredeemably awful ... and that is something no-one wants to hear. Here we find ourselves at the heart of the marginal ideology: the embarrassing realisation that we all *naturally* go about marginalising other people. It would seem, therefore, that this small matter of sexual awareness, which traditionalists would have us play down, *actually flags up what the story is all about.*

Expulsion as Punishment

The end of the story is complex. First, Yahweh distributes three curses: one to the serpent, another to Eve and a final one to Adam himself. Then he explains that Adam and Eve can't be allowed to stay in the Garden since they might eat the fruit of the tree of life and so become immortal. Finally, he actually expels Adam and Eve, taking precautions so that they can never return. Given the authoritarian framework they are working with, tradi-tionalists summarise all of this under the rubric of *punishment*. They claim the story as a whole describes the phenomenon of punished disobedience which can best be summarised by the phrase 'Man's Fall'. Indeed, for them the story sets the scene for what they claim is to follow, namely salvation and restoration: the job Jesus supposedly carried out on the cross. Such reductionism is not just a pitiful way in which to treat this magnificent story, it also runs roughshod over it in a most brutal and illogical way. For the whole point of the story's ending is to make it absolutely clear that there is no question of Man *ever* returning to Eden. If people find this hard to take I would ask them to look at the only other place where the writer mentions Yahweh's garden (Genesis 13.10). There he recounts that Abraham's nephew Lot chose to settle in Sodom because 'it was well watered and like the garden of the Lord'. If you want to find out what the writer thought would happen to people who, like the traditionalists, would foolishly try to return to Eden it is well worth reading the rest of that story.

Leaving such foolishness aside what can we make of the story's ending, using a marginal rather than an authoritarian approach? In order to highlight what needs explaining, let me put it to you like this: when Adam and Eve acquire moral awareness by eating the fruit why does Yahweh change his plans and force them to leave his garden for the big outside world where they now clearly belong? Well, from the author's point of view the big outside world is manifestly where the story *has* to end since the whole point of his myth is to explain the nature of *the present situation* (what is past simply constituting the explanation itself). Nevertheless, we can't avoid the question of Yahweh's motivation in the story. For traditionalists, the whole thing is a terrible inconvenience for, given their Fall (punishment-for-disobedience) scenario, Yahweh should have threatened Adam and Eve with curses and expulsion *from the very beginning*. This means that they have in a sense to pretend that that was indeed what happened even though they know very well it wasn't. However, even this does not get them completely off the hook because they still have to explain why the story employs two means (irreversible curses straight from Yahweh's mouth and a cherubim with a flaming sword flashing back and forth guarding the way) which together show that a return to the garden, with or without Jesus, is not on the cards. Since there can be no way of dealing with this problem, traditionalists characteristically ignore it. So let's consider what a marginal perspective has to offer.

Expulsion as a Gracious Act

In the alternative, marginal reading this story is seen to be about Man's fateful and, later assuredly half-regretted decision, to choose to live with consciousness. Given this scenario, Yahweh's decision to chase Adam and Eve into the big outside world can only be understood as an act carried out for their own good. But can the story be read in this fashion? There's an obvious advantage in such a reading since it squares perfectly with a return to the garden being out of the question. However, there is one major problem; the explanation the myth itself gives:

And the LORD God said, 'The man has now become like one of us, knowing good and evil. He must not be allowed to reach out his hand and take also from the tree of life and eat, and live forever.' (Genesis 3:22)

This is a very curious verse for a number of reasons:

- Though both trees are mentioned from the very beginning only one of them, the tree of the knowledge of good and evil, has played any role in the story so far. This makes me suspect the author introduced the tree of life simply to have an excuse for expelling Adam and Eve.
- The logic concerning this second tree does not really work for had it been there from the beginning Adam and Eve would assuredly have tasted its fruit. You could argue, I suppose, that its benefits only came about as a result of regular consumption but this would not have been the normal understanding, as can be seen from the Adapa

story where eating and drinking the bread and water of life *on one occasion* is seen as doing the trick.

- This verse is the only occasion on which the Bible mentions immortality, which is a superstitious belief. The quest for immortality fills ancient Near Eastern literature but is notably absent in the Bible. Indeed the writer of Genesis 2-3 makes nothing of this belief in his writings which strongly suggests he is only using it here as a ploy.

- The verse is not only a problem for those, like me, who argue for a marginal reading of the text. It is equally problematic for traditionalists since their punishment-based explanation does not square with this curious verse either.

- Taken at face value the explanation offered by this verse means not only that Yahweh is a died-in-the-wool authoritarian whose primary concern is to live without rivals but also that the serpent was an honest creature who told Eve nothing but the un-garnished truth. So if this verse is to be seen as representing the mythmaker's true beliefs *all of us* have a very real problem on our hands!

- Up till this point the mythmaker has shown that he operates with a firm grasp of reality. However, if we are to accept this verse as representing his true beliefs we will be forced to conclude that he has suddenly and inexplicably lost the plot.

You might be thinking I am telling you all this simply to prepare you for the shock of jettisoning the verse, but rest assured, the verse is important and certainly must stay! However, we have to put our minds to understanding what exactly is going on.

What's the Reason for the Prevarication?

If we follow our instinct that this is a marginal text then we have to believe the writer saw Yahweh as expelling Adam and Eve (and taking steps to ensure they never return) *for their own good*. Accordingly the writer must be making the point that Yahweh sees the garden as representing a danger of some sort for Adam and Eve. This is something he eventually makes explicit, as I have already indicated, in the story of Sodom and Gomorrah. It has to be understood that what we are talking about here is a danger that did not exist in the very beginning when Yahweh made the garden. It was rather a danger that had come about because of the fateful choice Adam and Eve had made. In other words, what the writer has to try and say is that while it was OK for Adam and Eve to live in the garden when, like the other animals, they were without consciousness, it is now no longer safe for them to do so. But why did he never say this and why did he instead palm-off his immortality explanation on us? Before we try to answer this question we must first find out why he thought the garden was no longer safe. What, to his mind, was the danger the garden supposedly represented to conscious animals like us?

Why was the Garden a Danger for Man?

It has to be said that the writer includes very little in his story for us to go on apart from the way in which he vaguely links this danger with sexual and therefore ideological awareness. So it is fortunate that later on in the story of Sodom and Gomorrah he is a little more forthcoming. There he makes it clear that he sees the leisured and indeed civilised garden situation as being closely connected with the pernicious centrarchical ideology he is fighting against. He does this by linking Sodom, the part of the country where Lot had foolishly decided to settle, not just with the garden situation in Eden but also with the garden situation in Egypt. From this we can tell that the mythmaker was conscious of the fact that the arrival of awareness itself, when linked with a leisured environment, inevitably exposed Man to pernicious centrarchical influences or, as we would say, the dangers of a hierarchical ideology. Now, the fact that the writer clarifies his thinking by linking the garden situation in Eden with the garden situation in Egypt begins to explain the major difficulty he was facing. It was easy for him to link what he would have considered as pernicious centrarchical ideas with Egypt, since everyone was aware that Egypt constituted the ideological enemy. However, linking *Yahweh's garden* with centrarchical ideas was quite another matter and a dreadful embarrassment.

Had he been able to say, as we so easily can, that 'Yahweh's garden started off by being good but later, with the arrival of consciousness, it become bad for Man in his new aware state' there would have been no problem. But his lack of psychological vocabulary made this quite impossible. All he could have indicated was that Yahweh's garden was bad, leaving it up to people to see the point. That, for obvious reasons, he simply could not bring himself to do but he simply had to find a way of getting Man out of the garden and into the outside world where the story inevitably had to finish. So he solved his problem, naturally enough, by taking refuge in the Mesopotamian myth from which he was working. He simply used its idea of immortality as a ploy, even though the subject was of no interest to him. At first you will almost certainly find this explanation strange, not to say scarcely credible, because we have no problem in talking about such things as awarenesses. However, I hope you will see that it explains what we find in the text very well and … just perhaps … you will end up agreeing with me.

3

Cain (Genesis 4)

The God of the Marginals Marks His Man

A Story of Two Brothers or a Story of a Man who Kills his Brother?

Most people, including scholars, think the story of Cain and Abel is about two brothers, one who was a farmer and the other a shepherd; but this is not the case. The name Abel, meaning ephemeral, makes it perfectly clear his role is simply to get blown away. This means the story is not about two brothers who, as a result of economic diversification, become rivals. Rather it is a story about a man called Cain *who becomes a marginal* as a result of killing his brother.

An Introduction to the Flood or a Completely Separate Story?

People sometimes try to understand this myth as an explanation of how it was that by the time Noah came along things had deteriorated so badly that Yahweh found it necessary to destroy the whole world. You see, traditionalists explain that Adam and Eve's sin (in eating 'the forbidden fruit') was a bigger deal than it might at first seem because, they will tell you, it was done in flagrant disregard of Yahweh's command. However, even they realise that it is fanciful to suggest that this single act of disobedience was, of itself, enough to justify the enormity of what was to come; namely the drowning of everybody and everything. So, these traditionalists have to try and find an explanation for God's anger somewhere else. The natural place to look then, is in the curious incident in Genesis 6.2 concerning the marriage of the sons of God (Nephilim) with the daughters of men, since this seems like a natural introduction to the story of the flood. For my money this verse does indeed offer a perfectly satisfactory reason as to why it became necessary for Yahweh to destroy humanity. However, others find it ambiguous which means they feel it necessary to find an alternative explanation from elsewhere. So, given its bridging position between the Adam and Eve story and the story of The Flood, they see it as falling to the story of Cain to produce the necessary account of humanity's violent downward spiral into hopeless moral degradation.

Cain the World's Worst Criminal

Given this point of departure it is hardly surprising that a great deal of time and ingenuity has been spent in trying to dig up as much dirt as possible about poor old Cain. For example, from the fact that in the genealogy that follows the story Cain is said to be the ancestor of a tribe of wandering blacksmiths who, as well as making such things as knives and forks and pots and pans, presumably also made weapons, it has been argued that Cain himself must therefore be seen as some sort of warmonger! Whenever you find people striving to explain the central feature of a biblical story by working on its details, as here, you can be certain ... absolutely certain ... they are up to no good.

I have to say I find all of this quite amazing since it seems to me perfectly clear what the story of Cain is saying and it has nothing ... absolutely nothing ... to do with what caused the flood. So, let us have a careful look at it, keeping our eyes firmly fixed on the central thrust and avoiding the temptation to delve into its details.

The Story Baldly Put

As a result of rivalry created by economic diversification, Cain ends up by killing his brother. This makes him a pariah in the community in which he lives, as Yahweh (Cain's conscience) points out. So Cain is forced to become a marginal living in the land of Nod, a mythical place of utter despair where there are no prospects since nothing grows. (What a marvellously succinct and evocative way this is of bringing to mind the condition of the marginal. I find it deeply moving. However, I imagine that to appreciate it fully you would have to be a marginal yourself). Contemplating his fate, Cain is inconsolable. He cries out in anguish that it is more than he can bear. Yahweh is driving him out of the community to a place where he will be forgotten even by Yahweh himself. To cap it all there is the very real prospect that anyone who finds him will kill him in revenge.

Yahweh Reveals Himself as the God of the Marginals

In later accounts concerning the patriarchs (Abraham, Isaac and Jacob) the writer of this story often describes moments when a character he is talking about suddenly finds him/herself marginalised and it is always at such moments that Yahweh appears, thereby showing that, as the god of the marginals, he is *his/her* god. This is precisely what happens here. Yahweh begins by telling Cain he couldn't be more wrong in thinking he will be forgotten. To make his point unmistakably clear he proceeds to put his mark on Cain, *showing that as a marginal* Cain is now his personal property, which hadn't been the case previously when Cain had been an honest and law-abiding person with a place in society like everyone else. This is a point which law-abiding folk with a place in society seem to find quite unacceptable for they either avoid it or else explain it away in any number of different and ingenious ways. However, their problems are not over for there is more to come!

Cain-Killers to get the Maximum

Doomfully, Yahweh then declares that anyone who dares to take revenge on Cain will be punished ... and not just severely punished but punished with the maximum sentence imaginable: death seven times over. Later, in Cain's genealogy, one of his murderous distant grandsons is described as attempting to outdo this by suggesting that anyone who takes revenge on him will get the death sentence seventy-seven times over. This is a bit over the top but it does emphasise the point being made: that there is nothing, but *nothing* in the whole wide universe that is worse than attacking a marginal, *for marginals belong to Yahweh as god of the marginals.*

Cain's Murder of his Brother as an Ordinary Offence

Now, in his writings the author of this piece speaks of two types of sin. First there is what could be called *ordinary* sin which never merits the death penalty and second there is what could be described as *ideological* sin, or rebellion against Yahweh, which invariably merits the death penalty. As I have previously said, much study has gone into analysing the Cain story as an explanation of how it was that Man's violent downward spiral into complete moral degradation led to Yahweh's decision to destroy the world. Inevitably this has lead to the conclusion that Cain's sin was the worst kind imaginable. At the same time little or nothing has been made of the sin of those who would have taken revenge on Cain, apart from saying that it is wrong to take the law into your own hands and that revenge is harmful as a motivation. I find this situation extraordinary because in the story it is manifestly clear that Yahweh *does not punish Cain,* which must make his sin, according to the writer's own criteria, *ordinary,* whereas Yahweh clearly threatened those who would take revenge on Cain with the maximum penalty! Just think about that for a minute!

Cain is Not Even Punished

I am aware people will object to what I have just written, pointing out that in Genesis 4:13-14 Cain specifically says:

My punishment is more than I can bear. Today you are driving me from the land, and I will be hidden from your presence; I will be a restless wanderer on the earth, and whoever finds me will kill me.

Doesn't this mean that Yahweh punishes Cain by banishing him? Well, no it doesn't. Punishment is an authoritarian act that adds a supplementary woe to the suffering already experienced by a criminal whose crime has been uncovered. If you read verses 11 and 12 carefully you will see that Yahweh does not punish Cain with banishment. As I have indicated above he simply spells out the inevitable consequences of Cain's act, given that it has become public knowledge: for now, of course, Cain cannot remain in the community with all the exchanges with neighbours that this implies. In our society we would have dealt with the matter by putting Cain in prison but there were no prisons in those days. Consequently, discovery of his crime itself renders Cain a marginalised outcast. Being civilisation-people and conse-quently judging Cain to be beyond the pale, we have generally accepted that the Hebrew word describing Cain's appalling predicament is 'punishment'. However, it's interesting that the English Standard Version of the Bible has a footnote saying that the Hebrew word used means 'guilt' and other translations propose 'shameful condition', 'wickedness' or 'iniquity'[9]. So Cain is not punished by Yahweh. However, as we have just seen, law-abiding folk (like us) who would take revenge on people like Cain most certainly are threatened with punishment, and how!

As Usual the Revisionist Editor has the Last Word

Interestingly the priestly writer of Genesis 1 seems to have been just as appalled by the terrifying point being made by the Hebrew myth-maker. He was most probably one of the adminis-trators of the post-exilic community, a government official working on behalf of his Persian overlords with responsibility for good order. So it's natural he couldn't accept the myth-maker's point that god-fearing civilisation-folk who take revenge on Cain are a thousand times more guilty than the marginal himself. Because of this he lost no time in inserting a corrective in Genesis 9:6:

> Whoever sheds the blood of man,
> by man shall his blood be shed;
> for in the image of God
> has God made man.

What we find here is the time honoured, conservative, 'image of god' formulation, along with its wretched, authoritarian, civilisational perspective, used to cover up and obscure the mythmaker's mind-blowingly important, marginal stance. Need I say more?

The Sacrifice of Isaac (Genesis 22:1-14)

The Marginal Strategy Which Offers No Guarantee

A Truly Amazing Story

Of all the stories in the Bible the sacrifice of Isaac is surely the strangest. The reason I say this is twofold. On the one hand, for centuries its power over the human imagination has been proved again and again, which means that it now stands as one of the most memorable and powerful stories in our civilisation ... on a par with any of them and greater than most. However, on the other hand, it has to be said that no truly satisfactory explanation as to what it actually means has yet been given. It's quite amazing!

The Priestly Editors' Line

People will protest that what I say here is not true since the meaning of the story is made explicit in the very first line. In 'testing' Abraham, as the story claims, Yahweh was clearly insisting on an absolute and over-riding need for blind obedience in his servants ... conservative blind obedience that is. I am perfectly willing to admit that this is how the Bible's conservative priestly editors wanted people to read the story since such an authoritarian line is all too clearly the overarching way in which they wanted people to read *all of these Genesis stories*. But does such an authoritarian reading truly fit the story itself? There are a number of reasons for saying it doesn't.

Doubts about this Conservative Thesis

- In the first place, read as the story of a straightforward encounter between Yahweh and Abraham, it's hard not to see Yahweh as justifying child sacrifice since it is the one thing he demands from Abraham. This is highly problematic, not just because child sacrifice is a practice we all find repugnant (to put it mildly) but also because it is a practice which the tradition later rejected and even used as a way of highlighting the kind of faithless conduct that finally brought down old Israel. There has been a lot of argument about whether Yahweh countenances child sacrifice in the Bible, as the story seems to suggest (a point we will be dealing with in a minute) but the existence of the argument itself is bizarre since it indicates that there is an underlying lack of clarity which really should not exist. For surely there should be no doubt at all that God is against child sacrifice?

- Secondly, laying aside this moral issue for a moment, it could be said that the storyteller is simply using child-sacrifice as the most extreme form of personal sacrifice conceivable. There is a lot to be said for seeing the sacrifice of your child as the biggest possible sacrifice you can make, next to that of sacrificing your own life. So it's not difficult to see the logic of using such a sacrifice as a telling way of making the point about the necessity for blind obedience. However, Abraham's preparedness to sacrifice his own life would have made the same point much better since it would have avoided the terrible moral issue of sacrificing someone else's life.

- The third reason for being sceptical about this conservative and authoritarian 'blind obedience' reading of the text is that it severely reduces the story's stature. All conservative elites in the ancient world wanted people to blindly obey and all of them told stories in a roundabout way to this effect. Nevertheless, none of them did it as brazenly as the biblical editors would have us believe this story does. Blind obedience means giving up your human responsibility and, without that, a life is no longer truly a life. This means that there is a dreadful lack of sophistication in the way in which this text supposedly shoves blind obedience baldly in your face; the exceptional circumstances only serving to highlight the third-rate nature of the whole conservative enterprise. For what on earth is there to be said of blind obedience if it involves giving up your life, let alone the life of your son?

Jewish Explanations

Because of the huge moral problems involved in commanding Abraham, for whatever reason, to sacrifice his son it's hardly surprising that Jewish exegetes over the centuries invented any number of ingenious strategies to protect Yahweh from blame, none of which, unfortunately, could be made to square with the text which, because of its uncompromising baldness, leaves no room for such devices. (See Wikipedia)

Christian Explanations

Christian exegetes, for their part, had an added problem for they wanted to see the text as somehow involving Jesus. Since Jewish commentators had already argued that, at the time, Isaac was already a fully grown man, thus implying that the incident involved not just Abraham's faith but also Isaac's willingness to be sacrificed, it was easy to argue that Isaac's 'self-sacrifice' prefigured Jesus' death on the cross. An alternative way of performing the same trick was to see the ram, which in being sacrificed became the substitute for Isaac's humanity, as prefiguring what Jesus eventually did for all humanity. Yet a third way of achieving the same end was to argue that, just as Abraham showed a willingness to sacrifice his son in deference to God's unexplained but presumed higher purposes, so too God showed a willingness to sacrifice his own son in order to save the world from sin (whatever that means).

More recently, it has become fashionable to argue that, when properly understood, far from countenancing child sacrifice the story actually advocates its abolition. However, like all of the above evasions this thesis founders on the rock of the story itself. For the story builds its logic on child sacrifice as a well known current practice about which it has nothing to say either for or against. People try desperately to argue that the story makes the point that *child sacrifice is no longer necessary;* but nothing could be further from the truth. All the story actually says is that on this particular occasion child sacrifice proved to be unnecessary *since the objective was only to prove Abraham's willingness to go through with it.* I find it amazing people persist with such a painfully silly idea, for who on earth would construct a story designed to attack the practice of child sacrifice by beginning it with God demanding a child sacrifice on his own behalf?

Child Sacrifice: The Evidence

If we want to understand what the story is about we will have to start by putting all of these evasions aside and allow it to speak for itself. Since it builds its logic on child sacrifice, a practice we have fortunately never experienced, we had better start by finding out what child sacrifice involves. There is very little actual archaeological evidence for the practice in the ancient Near East. Written evidence, on the other hand, is quite extensive though historians warn that one should take such evidence with a pinch of salt since it was easy to denigrate your enemies by wrongly accusing them of such a woeful practice. The Bible itself makes many references to the subject:

- Joshua 6:26-27 where Joshua, having just sacked the city of Jericho, curses it in Yahweh's name, saying that it will only be possible to rebuild after performing a number of child sacrifices.
- 2 Samuel 21:4-9 where David performs child sacrifices

(hanging seven of Saul's sons) to take away the curse of famine which was brought about by Saul's wanton slaughter of the Gibeonites.

- 1 Kings 16:33-34 where in the days of King Ahab a certain Hillel of Bethel rebuilds Jericho after sacrificing his eldest and youngest sons to ward off Joshua's terrible curse made in Yahweh's name.(see above)

- 2 Kings 3:26-27 where the Moabite king who is being besieged by the combined forces of Israel and Judah, in desperation offers up his eldest son as a burnt offering on the wall of the city, the result being the dispersal of his enemies who are forced to withdraw.

- 2 Kings 16:2-3 where King Ahaz offers his son as a burnt sacrifice, here categorised as an abominable practice of the other nations whom Yahweh had driven out of the land.

- 2 Kings 17:7 where it is said that in the days of King Hoshea (the last king of Israel) the people burned their sons and their daughters as offerings, and used divination and sorcery and sold themselves to do evil in the sight of the Lord, provoking him to anger.

- 2 Kings 21:6 where it is said that Manasseh, king of Judah, burned his son as an offering, and practiced soothsaying and augury, and dealt with mediums and with wizards. He did much evil in the sight of the LORD, provoking him to anger.

- 2 Kings 23:10 where it is said that Josiah, king of Judah, took steps so that 'no-one would make a son or a daughter pass through fire as an offering to Molech'.

- Jeremiah 7:30-35 and 19:3-5 where the prophet criticises the people of Judah in the name of Yahweh for burning 'their sons in the fire as burnt offerings to Baal, which I did not command or decree, nor did it come into my mind.'

- Ezekiel 16:20-21 and 20:30-31 where the prophet criticises the people of Judah for making child sacrifices to foreign gods and idols (see also Psalms 106:37-39) and in 20:25-26 where he very strangely seems to imply that Yahweh only commanded them to make child sacrifices to him in order 'to horrify them'.

The Essence of Child Sacrifice

Even taking into account the historians' appeal for scepticism, these passages seem to indicate a common thread; namely that child sacrifice existed in Israel and Judah, not as a common occurrence but as an unusual act carried out by leaders who, finding themselves in political extremis eventually broke down and in desperation resorted to magic, with human sacrifice being the most extreme form of this magic. For example, in 2 Kings 3:26-27 the Moabite king who is being besieged by the combined forces of Israel and Judah, in desperation offers up his eldest son as a burnt offering on the wall of the city. As a result of this powerful act of magic his enemies are forced to withdraw.

No sign of coercive magic in this story

That then is the intrinsic nature of child sacrifice, whether it is found in the Bible or in any other ancient Near Eastern texts: *a desperate act of magic which political leaders sometimes resort to as a last measure when all real hope is lost*. However, the surprising thing is that there is nothing of this 'desperate resorting to magic' anywhere in Genesis 22 which simply recounts that one fine day Yahweh told Abraham to go and sacrifice his son. It's as bald as that. Yahweh never attempts to explain why such a sacrifice is necessary. What's more, Abraham never asks him for such an explanation or even wonders to himself 'what's the score!' It's really quite mind-blowing when you think about it. So if Genesis 22 is indeed a story about child sacrifice, as commentators ancient and modern, Jewish and Christian, seem to agree, then all I can say is that it breaks every rule of storytelling for it bears no comparison with any other story of child sacrifice that I know of.

This is one of those facts which, once you recognise it, changes everything and it makes me wonder why others haven't noticed it.

A Representation not a Story

The truth is that Genesis 22 cannot possibly have originally been a story about child sacrifice, at least in the way in which we normally use this word *story*, which is to say as a recital of something that happened, whether in real life or only in the imagination (as in novels or fairy stories). It cannot have been that sort of story because it makes no sense understood as such. It can only have been an allegory or *representation* of some description. This should hardly surprise us since most of the texts in the Patriarchal cycle (Genesis 12:34) are clearly represen-tations, which is the reason why they too make no sense when people mistakenly try to understand them as stories. For example, take the story of Lot (Genesis 19). Here we are told of Lot's two daughters having sex with their father because there were no other men about. What kind of sense can you make of that? No men in central Palestine! Then again take the story of Jacob and Esau (Genesis 25). It begins by telling us about two babies who spent their time struggling with each other in their mother's womb in order to be the first to emerge! What sort of a story is that ... a likely story wouldn't you say?

OK. So these are not meant to be understood as ordinary stories. But why do I say that they are in fact *representations?* Well they are quite obviously presented as representations since all the important males in them are said to represent communities. The patriarchs themselves represent Israel while Abraham's oldest son, Ishmael represents the Ishmaelites. Lot's grandsons, Moab and Ammon, represent the Moabites and the Ammonites while Esau, Jacob's elder brother, represents the Edomites. Since all of these stories are clearly about communities, not individuals, they can only have been meant to be taken as representations dealing with Israel's political relationships with the surrounding peoples. Once we understand this all of the previously insurmountable problems simply fall away for the moral questions raised by child sacrifice become irrelevant, seeing that we are no longer dealing with a child sacrifice but rather with the thing which 'child sacrifice' here represents ... whatever that may be.

Representations as Necessary for Communication

Did I hear you sigh? I know people tend to be turned off by this business of representations, finding it unnecessarily complicated. What we have to remember is that when it came to political discussion these ancient writers were very restricted in the way in which they could talk about such matters. We are used to dealing with sophisticated political concepts which makes it easy for us to talk about the relationships between communities; say between the English and the French. But they could only do so by telling stories in which such communities were represented by individuals. So if we want to understand what they were saying we will have to learn to read their representational stories correctly.

Isaac as Yahweh's Promise

Let's take things one step at a time. We already know that in this story, as in all the others, we are dealing with Israel's understanding of her task in transforming the world, given her political perspective as a community of Hebrew marginals. We also know that Abraham represents Israel herself. The first thing we have to do therefore is find out what Isaac represents. As Abraham's son, Isaac must surely represent Israel's future but, interestingly, this is not the way the texts themselves express it. In the text this *future* is always spoken about as *Yahweh's promise*. It's also interesting that Yahweh's promise is always either represented by the Patriarch's *wife*, as in the story of Abraham and Sarah in Egypt (in

Genesis 12) or by the Patriarch's *younger son,* as in this story here. But why *younger* son? Well, it's obvious and ingenious isn't it? Younger sons were life's losers since once the elder son inherited they became extraneous. Consequently younger sons were the ideal representatives of the revolutionary Hebrew marginal tradition.

The Promise: the Vindication of the Hebrew Strategy

'That's all very well' I hear you murmur, 'Isaac may be Yahweh's promise. But what exactly is Yahweh's promise?' That's a very good question and to answer it we have to remind ourselves of the covenant agreement between Yahweh as the god of the Hebrew marginals and his people. To cut a long story short, this covenant agreement is all about a strategy for transforming (i.e. saving) the world. The agreement is that if Israel stands up for herself and boldly demonstrates what it means to be a community living together in radical solidarity (loving the neighbour as the self) thus allowing no-one to become marginalised, then Yahweh will vindicate her efforts and see her right ... by softening Gentile hearts; which is to say by seeing to it that they are shamed into changing their oppressive ways. Yahweh's promise, therefore, is simply his side of this covenant agreement: his promise to vindicate the Hebrew strategy. And this promise is consistently *represented* in all the Patriarchal stories as the desperately longed-for inheritor, which is to say the birth of the Patriarch's youngest male child.

The Promise is not an Assurance

If I say *desperately longed-for* birth it is because all of the Patriarchal stories insist that this promise to vindicate the Hebrew strategy is far from being something that comes to fruition as a matter of course, as is the case with normal human strategies built on coercion. For example, in a social revolution if the lower classes manage to organise themselves then they will almost inevitably succeed in overthrowing the much smaller ruling class. This, however, is not the case with the Hebrew strategy since it works by *shaming* not *coercion*. Therefore, for those who adopt the Hebrew strategy there can be no such assurance. *Hence the repeated accounts of the barrenness of the patriarch's legitimate wife representing the fact that Hebrew revolutionaries are forced to work with hope rather than certainty.* The point being made here, a devastatingly practical and worldly point, is that the softening of the Gentiles' hearts (vindication of the Hebrew strategy) is something that can only be hoped and longed for since it is an outcome that is not finally in the revolutionaries' hands.

Sacrificing the Promise as the Need to Continue Even when there is No Hope

But what can sacrificing Isaac as Yahweh's promise possibly mean?' Well, doesn't life teach us that it is but a fool's hope to believe that Gentiles' hearts can be softened by a mere demonstration of a better way of living? Doesn't this mean that to be a Hebrew revolutionary a person has to be prepared to go on not just without any real down to earth hope of success but also, at the end of the day, even without the comfort of this precious promise? Isn't that what all of these stories are about ... Yahweh strangely failing to fulfil his promise? That, therefore, was Abraham's test, as the one who represented faithful Israel: to be prepared to continue carrying out the Hebrew revolution even when it became clear there was no hope of it succeeding; the chances being that the Gentiles were never going to be shamed. That surely must be what the story is about, wouldn't you say?

Jesus and the Hebrew Strategy

So, that would appear to be the all too appalling truth and there is really nothing more to say except to consider how the story, with its perfectly terrifying strategy, relates to Jesus. All four evangelists present Jesus as deliberately bringing matters to a head by calling on his fellow Israelites to join him in a final effort to put this terrifying Hebrew strategy into effect. Instead of just playing at being faithful Israel, they would, together, jointly become Yahweh's light, as Second Isaiah had so brilliantly put it. Of course, all four evangelists then go on to relate that when it came to the crunch, everyone deserted Jesus leaving him to carry out this strategy alone. You could say, therefore, that Jesus faithfully carried out the terrifying Hebrew strategy right to the bitter end and that, in doing so, he *fulfilled* what this story of the sacrifice of Isaac talks about.

Of course it would not be fair to describe what the Hebrews achieved as just talk. However, I suggest it is fair to say they never managed to completely bridge the gap between talk and action. But isn't this precisely what the evangelists claim Jesus finally achieved on his journey to the cross:

Father, remove this cup from me. Nevertheless not my will but your will be done.(Luke 22:42)?

And isn't this why they describe him as crying out in despair as he was dying:

My God, my God, why have you forsaken me?(Mark 15:34)?

Wasn't this their way of saying Jesus finally succeeded in putting the Hebrew strategy into effect: 'sacrificing the promise' in being prepared to continue even when there was *no more room for any hope?* For me, the story of the sacrifice of Isaac is the greatest political story ever told, just as Jesus' death on the cross was the greatest political act anybody has ever achieved.

Expectations

I don't imagine you will actually like what this story says for who could like it? Indeed, I don't even expect you to decide to join the Hebrew revolution, however obvious it may be that it is the right thing to do. Nevertheless I do hope you will agree that, understood in this way, the story of the sacrifice of Isaac makes profoundly good sense... something it doesn't do at all when understood in the 'normal' way as just a story about a man and his son.

5

The Rape of Dinah (Genesis 34)

The Marginal Strategy Which Firmly Rejects Integration

The Setting

To properly appreciate this gem of a story you first have to know about its setting. It appears as the last of five stories in the Patriarchal cycle, where each story deals with Israel's political relationship with one of the communities making up her world[10]. This last story is all about the Israelites' relationship with the Canaanites.

As I have said before, at a time when little abstract vocabulary had been developed, biblical writers were in the habit of devising other mechanisms to facilitate the task of discussing political matters. One of these was to represent the political relationships between whole communities by telling stories about individuals. Another was to use *sexual* representations when discussing *ideological matters*. Thus, for example, if Israel is described by a biblical writer as whoring after foreign gods it does not mean that the nation began to make pilgrimages to foreign shrines so as to use the services of cult prostitutes. *It simply means that in adopting the dominating civilisational practices of her neighbours the community was beginning to become ideologically lax.* When reading this story you should bear this in mind and the fact that we are talking here about Israel's relationship with her nearest neighbours; namely the various civilisation-people they found already living in the region in which they had decided to settle.

A Difficult Text

This is known as one of the Bible's famous 'difficult passages' because of the problems experienced in interpreting it. What earns it this title is not the fact that the events described are hard to believe or difficult to understand but rather that the Israelites are said to have behaved in a particularly disgraceful manner ... at least by our modern standards. They begin negotiations very deceitfully and then cap it all by massacring or enslaving a whole community including innocent women and children.

A Source of Embarrassment

For atheists, of course, this demonstrates all too clearly the primitive nature of the Bible and shows how worthless it is as a standard now to live by. For Jewish or Christian believers the Israelites' reprehensible behaviour is a potential source of embarrassment ... something that has to be explained away, which is not easy. That said, modern day liberals find a clever way of immunising themselves. They make a virtue of standing loose to the Bible, reminding us that this Dinah text is after all 'just a story'. In this way they manage somehow to remain crypto-believers while at the same time agreeing with the atheists that the Bible is not to be taken too seriously ... especially when it does not countenance their own liberal opinions, as is invariably the case! I have to say, I find this approach decidedly shoddy even though it's easy to see why liberals cling to it, since it renders their position invulnerable ... which accounts for their characteristically laid-back air. However, unfortunately for them, the approach cannot possibly be justified, historically speaking. For if the Bible was just a collection of stories, which people were at liberty to interpret as they liked, there would be no way of accounting for the extraordinary impact it has had on people over the centuries or of explaining why it alone, of all the literary works from the ancient Near East, has endured as a motivating factor amongst people. I put it to you that if there is one thing we can say with absolute assurance about the biblical writers it is that they believed they had things of great importance to say about the human condition. Due to editorial interference and our own quite different perspectives and ways of expressing ourselves, we may not nowadays immediately see what these things 'of great importance' are but we have no justification whatsoever in writing off the biblical writers' work as 'just stories'. Instead let's do our best to work out what they were trying to say, regardless of whether we end up agreeing with them.

Ways of Dealing with It

Given that we must take the story of Dinah seriously what sense can be made of the Israelites' uncivilised behaviour? Some have tried to soften the problem by homing in on the fact that the text kicks off by describing Dinah as *Leah's* daughter and by telling us that she went out to visit the women of the land. Their suggestion is that in seeking to have relations with the Canaanites Dinah behaved imprudently, putting herself at risk ... something no daughter of *Rachel* would have done, or so the inference is. It's true that, in shovelling responsibility for the rape onto Dinah herself as the imprudent daughter of Leah, one can muddy the water and so to some extent reduce the discomfort engendered by the story. Indeed there is evidence that the priestly editors themselves had just such a strategy in mind. Notice, for example, how right up to verse 23 the participants are Jacob's sons and Dinah's brothers *in general*, making it quite clear that *all* Israel is involved. Then suddenly, in verse 24, when the dreadful deed is done, it's just Simeon and Levi, sons of Leah and thus Dinah's full brothers, who act. Moreover, in the final verse (29) Jacob specifically criticises these two sons, thus distancing himself, and so Israel, from their act ... a criticism that the editor himself, later on in Genesis 49:5-6, heavily underlines:

> Simeon and Levi are brothers—
> their swords are weapons of violence.
> Let me not enter their council,

let me not join their assembly,
for they have killed men in their anger
and hamstrung oxen as they pleased.
Cursed be their anger, so fierce,
and their fury, so cruel!
I will scatter them in Jacob
and disperse them in Israel.

The Futility of Such Devices

It would seem therefore that it is not just modern commentators who are embarrassed by the Israelites' uncivilised behaviour but that the priestly editors shared these feelings and that it was they who began the exercise in trying to distance Israel from the barbaric events described. However these attempts, both ancient and modern, are futile. For though the other sons of Jacob were not actually involved in the massacre they were not slow to profit from it:

The sons of Jacob came upon the dead bodies and looted the city where their sister had been defiled. They seized their flocks and herds and donkeys and everything else of theirs in the city and out in the fields. They carried off all their wealth and all their women and children, taking as plunder everything in the houses. (Genesis 34:27-29)

What is more, though Jacob was angry with his two sons it was not because as a civilised man like us he was disgusted by their barbarity. It was only for strategic reasons:

You have brought trouble on me by making me obnoxious to the Canaanites and Perizzites, the people living in this land. We are few in number, and if they join forces against me and attack me, I and my household will be destroyed. (Genesis 34:30)

The Story as Essentially Anti-Canaanite

From start to finish the author of the story takes it as read that the Canaanites are the ideological enemy. For him the only question is: what would be the best way for the Israelites to neutralise the Canaanites without jeopardising their own position? You could say therefore that for him the fate of the Canaanites, including their women and children, was not important. Does this mean that atheists are in fact right and that what we are dealing with here is a text, later softened by unhappy editors, which originally gloried in an act of wanton destruction carried out by anti-civilisation barbarians?

An Uncouth Primitive Tale?

If the writer of the original story was indeed a primitive barbarian, as atheists imply, wouldn't you expect this to show in the way he describes his civilisation-foes just as is the case today when, for example, you hear young Taliban tribesmen describing the behaviour of the Americans and British, as they see things. Very well, let's see how our ancient writer portrays his civilisation-enemies:

> Jacob's sons ... were shocked and furious, because Shechem had done an outrageous thing in Israel by sleeping with Jacob's daughter—a thing that should not be done. But Hamor said to them, "My son Shechem has his heart set on your daughter. Please give her to him as his wife. Intermarry with us; give us your daughters and take our daughters for yourselves. You can settle among us; the land is open to you. Live in it, trade in it, and acquire property in it." Then Shechem said to Dinah's father and brothers, "Let me find favour in your eyes, and I will give you whatever you ask. Make the price for the bride and the gift I am to bring as great as you like, and I'll pay whatever you ask me. Only give me the young woman as my wife." (Genesis 34:7-12)

Decidedly Not!

Perversely, could there be a more beautifully succinct description of tolerance in action, of the 'live and let live' philosophy we civilisation-folk, following the ancient Greeks, so much admire? It's true Shechem starts off badly but, finding out who Dinah is and falling in love with her, he admits his error and from then on behaves impeccably, just like a gentleman. How do you explain such a perceptive piece of writing except by admitting the shocking fact that the scribe, whoever he was, was perfectly aware of civilisation's virtues and had nothing to learn about human behaviour from civilised people like us? Given that the scribe could by no stretch of the imagination be called an uncouth barbarian, how is it that on the one hand he describes his enemies glowingly (in our civilised terms) while on the other hand he describes his own people as positively vile? And we can't avoid the issue by pretending that this is 'just a story', for manifestly it isn't. It's one of the most finely manicured pieces of writing in the whole Bible and that can only mean that the author was attempting to draw attention to what he thought was an extremely important political point. Of course, had the scribe been a Canaanite we would have perfectly understood what he was saying: that the Israelites were an untrustworthy bunch of godforsaken terrorists. But this was not the case. Indeed it is quite clear that the scribe was in fact a revolutionary Hebrew. Only this can explain why the priestly editors later felt obliged to modify and soften the story ... just as modern expositors continue to do.

The Story's Marginal Point

So let's read the story from the marginal perspective to see what transpires. As usual, once we do this everything falls into place and begins to make perfect, if uncomfortable, sense. We have already determined that like all the other Patriarchal stories this one is from start to finish ideologically anti-Canaanite. This being the case the point being made can only be that if Israel is truly intent on ridding the world of its odious privilege-seeking ways and hypocritical cover-ups she must not give way a single inch to the Canaanites, the hated ideological enemy in their midst. This means rejecting out of hand all talk of compromise *for the Canaanites are at their most dangerous precisely when they behave in a civilised manner*. For fairly obvious reasons this reading constitutes a subtlety which we civilisation-folk never twig since it paints us as the bad guys. For marginals, however, it is self-evident, the only problem being (as the story shows) how to put this point into practice without bringing the whole edifice of civilisation down on one's head.

6

Moses (Exodus – Numbers)

Folk Hero or Marginal Hero?

You will perhaps be surprised to find we are dealing with the *whole* of Moses' life in this study which means including any number of stories each of which could rightly be said to warrant an individual study of its own. However, given that our aim is to understand the Bible as politics it can sometimes be necessary to get a general overview of the material, which is what I propose to attempt to do here. In this study I am going to use George. W. Coats' book *Moses: Heroic Man, Man of God* (Sheffield Academic Press, 1988). Please don't be put off if you have never heard of Coats or by the feeling that his analysis may be out of date. We are talking politics and politics have changed relatively little since the late eighties and in biblical scholarship not at all! Coats' work is interesting in that he presents a serious and weighty liberal interpretation of the Mosaic texts and this makes him a great dialogue partner.

Coats' basic contention is that Moses is presented in the Exodus texts as an *apolitical folk hero*. To fully appreciate what he is proposing you have to bear in mind that the traditional way of reading the Exodus texts is to see Moses as the *conservative religious hero* as presented, for example, in Cecil B DeMille's film *The Ten Commandments*. What Coats as a regular historian is basically doing here is jettisoning this conservative intervening God who, as my friend Elizabeth Templeton says jokingly, pokes at his creation from time to time ... and replacing him with the non-intervening ground-of-our-being, Liberal God whose purpose is to inspire. With God, as it were, safely back in heaven (or underground!) Moses ceases to be the miracle-working religious hero of Cecil B De Mille's film (and, it has to be said, of the revisionist writer (P), the author of Genesis 1) and becomes instead the apolitical liberal folk hero who, in being inspired, himself inspires ... just as God does. But can Coats square this folk hero figure with what is actually found in the texts?

Moses as a baby in a basket

These are the introductory words of the Legend of Sargon I, conqueror of Mesopotamia in the twenty-fourth Century B.C.E.

> Sargon, the mighty king, king of Agade, am I.
> My mother was a changeling, my father I knew not.
> The brother(s) of my father loved the hills.
> My city is Azupiranu, which is situated on the banks of the Euphrates.
> My changeling mother conceived me, in secret she bore me.
> She set me in a basket of rushes, with bitumen she sealed my lid.
> She cast me into the river which rose not over me.
> The river bore me up and carried me to Akki, the drawer of water.
> Akki the drawer of water lifted me out as he dipped his ewer.
> Akki the drawer of water, took me as his son and reared me.
> Akki, the drawer of water, appointed me as his gardener.
> While I was gardener, Ishtar granted me her love,
> And for four and [.] years I exercised kingship.

In the beginning of Exodus chapter 2 the writer generally known as the Yahwist (J) who also wrote Genesis 2-3 (which we looked at in Study 2) describes the birth of Moses, the future Hebrew leader, in strikingly similar terms. Since in those days Sargon was the model *par excellence* of the centrarchical political hero, it is natural to suppose that the Yahwist wanted his readers to find in his work a portrait of the contrasting Hebrew/marginal hero. Coats recognises the striking parallels between the Sargon and

Moses birth narratives but specifically rejects this comparison. Because of his studied, apolitical approach Coats' work on the Moses narratives is, I believe, fatally flawed. For in ignoring the Yahwist's highly charged ideological comparison of Moses and Sargon, Coats fails to give due weight to the political qualities of the 'hero of the marginals' which I believe the texts themselves are expressly designed to highlight – and, no, I am not here surreptitiously breathing into the texts what I later want to find, for the baby Moses is specifically described as being a Hebrew (i.e. marginal) child in Exodus 2:6.

In the extant Sargon material the king is portrayed as ruthlessly opportunistic yet highly respectful towards the centrarchical ideology in place. As Coats says, he appears to have been a foreigner of humble origins whose family came originally from the northern hills of Mesopotamia. He managed by some means to find employment as a personal servant to the King of Kish. There he instigated a coup against his master and went on to conquer all Sumer and create an empire covering the whole of Mesopotamia. He must have been some man. One gets the impression that he was all that civilisation would expect a hero to be: patient yet bold, shrewd yet fearless, a fine strategist as well as a great leader of men. For, clearly, at critical junctures in his career he was able to act decisively, overcoming all opposition by his sheer audacity, courage and strength of will till at the end he stood alone and the world applauded! This is emphatically *not* the figure one encounters in the Moses texts, especially if one reads them with the same eyes and from the same civilisational perspective. Indeed I can't help feeling that the Yahwist intended the comparison with Sargon partly as a joke, for the Moses stories begin with the Hebrew hero's flight as a consequence of his disastrously ill-considered action in killing the Egyptian taskmaster and end with his abysmal failure to seize the occasion, when the opportunity occurred, to lead Israel victoriously into the promised land (Numbers 13 & 14). This state of affairs is surely not fortuitous.

Moses as a young adventurist; and the lesson of solidarity

The Moses narrative begins with his attempt to break out of the isolation imposed by his peculiar upbringing and to establish solidarity with his own people by slaying an Egyptian whom he came across casually beating a Hebrew slave. Though it is easy to sympathise with his motives, the natural course of events reveals that his strategy of meeting aggression with aggression was disastrous. Moses seeks to become a leader of his people but of course the persecuted marginals are not going to follow an Egyptian centrarch who for some unknown reason claims to be one of them, or to associate with someone who openly indulges in terrorism. Consequently, when he subsequently tries to intervene in a quarrel between two fellow Hebrews the aggressor betrays him to the authorities so that Moses is forced to flee the country. Here Coats, in my opinion, completely misses the point. Instead of judging Moses' act in killing the Egyptian aggressor to be a foolish bit of youthful adventurism (as anyone with a modicum of political nous or experience would do) he takes it as a selfless, heroic act! Likewise, instead of seeing the subsequent action of the Hebrew slave as a normal reaction, given the circumstances, he describes it as a tragic rejection of the heroic benefactor! In this way Coats demonstrates that he is just as politically naive and out of touch as was the young Moses. If Moses seeks a role as defender of his people, his action in killing the Egyptian is politically crass and if he has to flee for his life and go into exile he has only got himself to blame. Coats' determination to see Moses as an apolitical folk hero leads him to paint over and spoil the Yahwist's vastly more interesting political portrait. What the Yahwist is in fact doing in this opening section of his work is drawing the picture of the nascent political hero of the Hebrew marginals who has to yet to learn the painful lesson that *solidarity with the marginals is a serious business and not something that can be acquired by an act of youthful adventurism. Being a Hebrew is not simply a matter of birth but of a more serious political belonging.*

Moses as a reluctant revolutionary; and the lesson of partnership

Moses finds no peace in exile. His desire for a role to play in the liberation of his people has not deserted him and he dreams of returning to Egypt. However, he hasn't yet got over his painful and unforeseen rejection. The Yahwist plays out the resolution of this dilemma in his famous episode of the burning bush, in which God continually calls on Moses to return to Egypt and Moses repeatedly raises objection. I say objection in the singular because in fact it always amounts to the same hesitation: Given what happened the last time, what assurance can Moses have that things will be different now? Because Coats has excluded the idea that Moses' first intervention had been a mistake he can see none of this. Consequently he is obliged to find another explanation to account for Moses' hesitancy, a characteristic which even he admits can easily be mistaken for a very unheroic weakness. The idea he comes up with is that it is simply a literary device for including the Aaronic tradition:

> Moses' objection that he has a heavy mouth and no words should not be taken as a sign of literal physical handicap, or even as an element in a non-heroic or anti-heroic picture in the literature, but rather as a marker that sets up the reassurance. ... The objection does not suggest that a handicap belaboured the work of Moses. Nor does it suggest a literary construct designed to highlight Moses' heroic flaw. Rather it is a literary construct that introduces the Aaronic tradition into the Moses story (Coats, *Moses* p. 69)

This, surely, is a trivialisation of the Yahwist's art. Moses is deliberately portrayed as someone who is preoccupied by his own inadequacy, given the enormity of the task he is facing, and this is something which the storyteller means us to come to terms with. That said it is certainly true the text aims to set up a reassurance. However, a reassurance has little content unless it is seen *as a valid response to a justified fear*. Indeed it is the nature of the fear that dictates the character of the reassurance. Coats reduces the importance of the reassurance by leaving us to infer that Moses acts simply out of personal insecurity. In this way Yahweh's reassurance becomes little more than the sympathy expressed by an understanding parental figure faced with a 'child' who lacks self-confidence.

The true substance of Moses' hesitations is contained in what happened in the past: once bitten he is now understandably twice shy. In the light of his warranted political misgivings how does the statement that Yahweh will be with him provide a *valid* reassurance that this time round things will be different? The text answers this question with what becomes a crucial political principle in Israel's ideology: the idea that the power of the Hebrew god manifests itself in an intimate, on-the-level *partnership* with the excluded marginals. Let me explain: the classical centrarchical idea concerning the manifestation of a god's power is that it has to be *mediated*. In Semitic culture it was believed that the power of a deity is such that too close a contact with a god or goddess results in the death of the humans concerned. They are burnt up by the godly presence. In other words the power of a centrarchical god or goddess is conceived of as essentially foreign and dangerous to human beings and can only be put at their disposal when properly mediated by centrarchical officials: the priests, and their chief, the king himself. The image of the bush that burns but is not consumed is therefore a direct contradiction of this centrachical understanding and conveys to Moses the antithetical way in which Yahweh's power functions as compared with that of all other deities[11].

Of course the centrarchs' contention that by using the correct mediatorial performances they were able to tap into the unseen forces of the universe was a charade. The power they exploited did not in fact come from such sources but rather from the human sweat and labour which they had purloined. As John Bright pointed out long ago (*The History of Israel* SCM Press 1960 p.161) the centrarchical gods were effectively no more than a justification of the *status quo*. The centrarchs established a centre of power, selected a god and set him or her up as the guarantor of their authority. I speak somewhat loosely here because, of course, in reality their choice was usually a foregone conclusion since the tribal god of the victorious group in power would invariably be given the job: in Sargon's case the god of the people of Agade who adopted him. In other words the power of a centrarchical god is really nothing more than the power which the leaders of a community have managed to draw into its centre by forcing dependency upon the people round about them: 'You give up your responsibility and a major portion of your labours and in return we will exert authority and offer you protection'. Such a power may be substantial, depending on the area controlled. However, it is essentially man-made or, more correctly, man-collected. In the words of the Israelites, the centrarchs' deities were in reality nothing more than worthless idols.

What Moses with his partnership principle did was to challenge this centrarchical, collected power by pitting against it the power of the god of the marginals; that power which liberates human potential as opposed to stealing it. As I have suggested, instead of working by persuading people to give up their power and then collecting and exploiting it ostensibly on their behalf, the marginal's god operates, as Moses sees it, to liberate the natural potential present in human beings by offering to work in partnership with them as their encourager and guarantor[12]. Unlike the power of the centrarchical deities this power is not man-made but the power of life itself[13]. Furthermore it is a power which is not exploitable after the manner of the centrarchs for it cannot be abstracted from the human beings it inhabits. Indeed it is a kind of power that can only be tapped by those who advocate independence and self-reliance. It is the contention of the biblical writers that the only people truly open to this power are those excluded from civilisation (e.g. Amos 3.1). Yahweh is *by definition* god of the marginals because only they are in a position to fully appreciate him and not because of their proactive strength, for they have none, but because of their weakness.

It now becomes apparent how Yahweh's reassurance works. His promise that he, the partnership god, will be with Moses if he returns to Egypt, leads Moses to understand that things *will* be different this time round since (to use the wording of the later prophets) he will be putting himself into the hands of the living God and pitting Yahweh's enormous and contrary power (the power which unleashes the potential of free human spirits (e.g. Isaiah 34:4, 41:8-16, 44:1-8) against the power of the centrarchs' lifeless idols (the power of selfish theft and mindless coercion)). As regards the rest of the discussion between Yahweh and Moses, this is concerned with strategic questions. On the first occasion Moses made the huge political mistake of attempting to enter directly and personally into the conflict with an act of blatant coercion. This time his strategy is to work through solidarity with the Hebrew community.

Moses as failed negotiator; and the lesson of hardening

Moses has little trouble in persuading the Hebrew leadership to let him negotiate with the Egyptians on their behalf. However, his efforts merely result in the authorities turning the screws down even harder, and the Hebrew foremen start to blame him for making the peoples' condition worse rather than better. According to Coats this well known *hardening* motif in the plague stories (time and time again Moses and Aaron do their stuff but the net result is always that Pharaoh hardens his heart) serves simply to emphasise the failure of Moses' efforts. He maintains that the present text is made up of two separate traditions which have been woven together. First there is the *Moses heroic saga* in which negotiations with the Egyptians fail, causing Moses to change tactics and attempt to bolt with the people into the wilderness. Second there is the *story of Yahweh's mighty acts* which find their centre in the Passover story in which Moses plays a minimal part. Coats recognises that Moses' failure as a negotiator in the Moses saga may raise questions about his position as a folk hero in some peoples' minds; however he maintains, somewhat weakly I find, that this is not in fact the case:

> ...while this unit may not contribute new material to the image of Moses as hero, it does not detract from the thesis ... It would appear to me that the failure in the negotiations process would not detract from the heroic image. (Coats, *Moses* p. 87)

I accept the Moses saga probably did conclude with a change of tactics, for once it became clear the Egyptians were not going to accept the justness of the Hebrews' complaints and winning arguments there was really no option other than to make a mad dash through the desert to freedom. That said, Coats signally fails to adequately deal with the *heart-hardening/failure* theme in the Moses saga which he appears to view as something to be swept under the carpet. This hardening-of-hearts business figures prominently, later on in the call of Isaiah (Isaiah 6:10), in Jesus' parabolic approach (Mark 4:11-12) and again in a reverse, *heart-softening* mode, in the resurrection itself (see Study 15). All of this makes me think it is ideologically crucial and worthy of further examination.

Brevard S. Childs pointed out that the two sources (J) and (P) employ the hardening phenomenon in quite distinct ways. Here is a summary of his findings:

- In the first source J, written by the revolutionary writer of Genesis 2, the hardening is described as either something which just happens to Pharaoh (Pharaoh's heart was hardened) or as something which Pharaoh himself brings about (Pharaoh hardened his heart). The plagues are seen as signs designed to reveal to Pharaoh knowledge of Yahweh and the hardening is a negative reaction to these revelations and results in a failure of the strategy.

- In the second source P, written by the authoritarian conservative writer of Genesis 1, the hardening is most often described as something which Yahweh brings about (God hardened Pharaoh's heart). The plagues are not seen as revealing signs aimed at making Pharaoh aware but rather as signs of Yahweh's judgement. The hardening of Pharaoh's heart is a failure by design so that Yahweh has further opportunities to display judgement against him.

The curious thing is that though Childs adequately described these differing approaches he failed to identify the ideological difference underlying them. These ideological differences are signalled by the fact that whereas the Yahwist (J) in his text offers an account of *a reactive strategy at work* (the plagues being revealing signs designed to open Pharaoh's eyes to what he is doing) the priestly writer (P) in his text presents the events dressed up in *a proactive gloss* (the plagues being symbolic manifestations of Yahweh's judgement.) It's clear that the priestly writer has doctored the text for whereas the Yahwist's account reads like a straightforward story his account is plainly theatre: Pharaoh being the fall guy who gets beaten up time and time again, just like the poor old Sheriff of Nottingham in the story of Robin Hood. It is true, of course, that even in the Yahwist's account we experience problems in viewing the plagues in a realistic light, which makes it difficult for us to see them as operating as exposures (i.e. revealing signs designed to get

Pharaoh to see what he is doing). But this is only because of our post-Enlightenment mindset. Childs could be right in calling the Yahwist's plagues 'revelations of the knowledge of Yahweh' except that I'm not sure what this means. I suspect that like Coats, Childs sees Yahweh in a liberal fashion as the great heavenly inspirer. This being the case I would want it to be clear that the plagues represented demonstrations of the reactive, light-bearing power of the Hebrew marginal ideology.

I have to say I used to find these plague stories difficult to take (just like the miracle stories in the New Testament). Consequently I tried to discover scientifically acceptable ways of understanding them. For example, I toyed with the idea of explaining the Israelites' crossing of the sea in terms of low lying flood plains and unusual winds and tides etc. However, I have now, somewhat late in the day, come to realise that this whole approach is ridiculous because it involves reading the texts with my own post-Enlightenment mindset instead of with the pre-Enlightenment mindset of the people who actually wrote them. It seems obvious to me now that if I want to understand these Exodus stories I should see them as *representational descriptions* of a nascent political movement rather than as *analytical accounts.* So I propose that we should stop asking *what exactly happened* and instead start asking *what was the ideological and strategic significance of what happened.* When we do this the answers we get to our questions turn out to be much more informative.

For my money, what the Yahwist seeks to show is that the Hebrews' strategy depended on their having the colossal and unprecedented nerve (or 'cheek' as the Egyptians would have seen it) to stand up for themselves and expose the grave injustice which was being done to them. He admits, of course, that this in itself was not enough to bring about their liberation. Indeed, as I have already noted, he openly avows that the consequence of the Hebrews' complaint to Pharaoh was that the screws were turned down on them even harder. However, he claims that this hardening of the heart was of itself indicative that *the exposure was getting through.* You could say that *for the very first time in human history the authorities were being faced with the unpalatable truth about themselves and were having their true hypocritical natures revealed; and that as this process continued, the hardening of their hearts was accentuated, thereby revealing that the exposure was proving increasingly effective.*

The trouble was that, lacking the descriptive powers necessary for setting out the actual arguments and stratagems that Moses and Aaron employed in piercing the civilisation-rulers' hypocritical righteousness, the Yahwist found it difficult to demonstrate how the Hebrew leaders managed to make their telling exposures. The solution he came up with (as usual) was to indicate the unmasking strength of their arguments and strat-agems *symbolically*, using the concept of plagues which smote civilisation while leaving the Hebrew community quite untouched. In other words, what we have here is yet one more example of the Yahwist's representational techniques to add to the list.

My conclusion is that what we see in the priestly account of these *heart-hardening and failure* texts is a clear example of ideological revisionism in which the writer gets rid of the ideological god of the marginals, replacing him with his own conservative and religious alternative.

Moses as a weak leader and the lesson of self-reliance

The expectation of those who admire the Sargonic hero is that as soon as Moses' strategy has been vindicated and the pursuing Egyptians have been seen off, Moses will immediately set about establishing a strong central system of command in order to affirm his leadership. This, however, Moses signally fails to do and what follows is a litany of murmurings (Exodus 15:24, 16:2, 17:2) directed against a seemingly weak leader. Coats, whose main object is to establish the figure of Moses as the apolitical folk hero, has to find a way around this obstacle:

> The murmuring tradition, so it seems to me, is a relatively late narrative revision of an older tradition, converting an originally positive account of Israel's life under Mosaic leadership to a negative account of rebellion. The reason for this conversion is still a subject for debate (Coats, *Moses*, pp.109-10).

However, seen from a marginal point of view, the murmuring tradition, far from constituting an obstacle to heroism introduced by some hypothetical late editor, represents the ideological nub of the matter. Moses has brought the people out of Egypt. Now they have to develop a proper self-reliance, away from its unhealthy, centrarchical culture of dominance and dependence. The narrative tells what a hard experience it was and how difficult the Israelites found it to shake free from their old ways. They cry out for centrarchical leadership from Moses, desiring to be relieved of the responsibility of looking after themselves, and when this is not forthcoming complain bitterly that they were better served even as slaves in Egypt. Moses for his part has considerable trouble in resisting their pressure and if he is to be accounted a hero it is surely in that he manages to do so, against the odds.

So if I have a problem with this story it is not in understanding why it depicts Moses as a weak leader from our civilisational point of view. That I find easy to grasp. What puzzles me is why it described Yahweh as giving in to the Israelites:

> And Moses said to them, "Why do you find fault with me? Why do you put the Lord to the proof?" ... And he called the name of the place Massah and Meribah, because of the fault-finding of the children of Israel, and because they put the Lord to the proof by saying, "Is the Lord amongst us or not?"

(Exodus 17:7 See Deuteronomy 6:16)

Logic would seem to dictate it would have been better if Yahweh had refused to go on 'saving' the people and instead had instructed them to stir themselves and set about finding solutions to their problems themselves. One has to assume the Yahwist found this an unacceptable storyline because he wanted to portray Yahweh as behaving consistently in the matter of salvation. He could not have Yahweh sometimes agreeing to save Israel and sometimes not since that would undermine his character as the god of the marginals. Whatever the case may be it is clear that the Yahwist sees the Israelites as sinful when they behaved as if their agreement to follow Moses into the wilderness put them in a position of having a call on God when things went wrong. The Yahwist describes this attitude as manipulative: 'putting Yahweh to the proof'. Instead of continuing to act responsibly in the belief that Yahweh would surely vindicate the 'marginal revolution' *in his own time and in his own way*, the Israelites abandon responsibility and demand that Yahweh, who got them into this mess, must now get them out of it. At its heart this is a superstitious attitude since it is a denial of the reality that we have no control over the forces which govern the universe. It is also a return to the centrarchical way of thinking in which human responsibility is sold in return for the right of protection, in the belief that the central authority is in the best position to influence the situation. Of course, we see the problem of superstition in our own post-Enlightenment way, as a denial of science. The Yahwist clearly saw it somewhat differently: as a denial of Yahweh's lordship. But, in fact, it all comes down to the same thing in the end: the need to take responsibility for one's actions and live life seriously, refusing to play silly games of pretence.

Moses' indecision and success in
lacking decisiveness

From the viewpoint of civilisation (we hero-worshipers of Sargon) Moses' weakness as a leader is most clearly visible in the indecision he displays when the opportunity arises to lead the people triumphantly into the promised land (Numbers Chs.13 & 14). This unit, which presents itself as the culmination of the murmurings tradition, depicts the return of the Israelite spies who have been sent to investigate Canaan. Their account of the promised land itself is unambiguous. They describe it as 'flowing with milk and honey' but, when it comes to assessing Israel's prospects of capturing it, most urge retreat since 'the people who dwell in the land are strong, and the cities fortified and very large'. Only two of their number, Joshua and Caleb, remain firmly positive and urge the community on. However, the people suffer a serious loss of nerve and Moses, in sharp contrast to Joshua and Caleb, offers them no leadership. As a result, Yahweh pronounces that of all the adult Israelites, including Moses, only Joshua and Caleb will survive to enter the promised land.

Once again Coats registers this as a problem to be surmounted as regards his Mosaic folk hero image:

The tradition about the death of Moses cannot be taken in itself as an indication of a reflex in the tradition designed to diminish the importance of Moses. Perhaps to attribute Moses' failure to enter the land to a sin at the spring of Meribah and thus to God's explicit denial of Moses' right, is to be understood as an effort to diminish the authority of Moses. But significantly, the statement about Moses' sin comes from the priestly source with its tendency to non-heroic forms of the Moses tradition. The Yahwist reports nothing of Moses' sin at Meribah. Those texts in Deuteronomy that emphasise Moses' sin and the consequent denial of right for Moses to enter the land (1:37, 3:26f, 4:21f) show the sin to be heroic.

> Moses did what he did 'because of you', because of his
> people. (Coats, *Moses* p.202)

Given its dramatic importance in the text I find it amazing that
Coats treats the inglorious death of Moses and his failure to
reach the promised land as a problem. Surely it's something to be
understood not something to be explained away, for all the signs
are that it has great symbolic significance. This being the case, we
have to ask ourselves what a physical entry into the promised
land constitutes in the story. The answer is surely unambiguous.
Entry into the promised land constitutes the *success* of the enterprise. In other words, by denying Moses a share in this
experience the Yahwist is deliberately denying him a share in
this success.

For a centrarchical hero like Sargon, success of this sort is
everything since it is his god's fundamental stamp of approval.
Consequently, the subsequent failure of his empire, even though
it occurs long after his death, constitutes the tragic flaw that
centrarchical civilisation-man sees as accompanying all human
endeavour. In the case of Moses, however, success in these
normal, civilisational terms is irrelevant. Israel declares him to be
her hero - the hero of the marginals - precisely because, in the
classic manner of all marginals, he loses his nerve at the critical
moment and so has no share in the promised land. In other
words, in moving from Sargon to the Moses story the idea of
what constitutes success and failure dramatically changes. If
Moses' life is judged to be a resounding 'success' it is not because
he shows himself to be capable of seizing the moment and
bringing his people final victory; because he doesn't. It is rather
because he never gives in by taking the normal and thus, easy
route and making himself Israel's centrarch. Here in this
ideological matter his nerve holds surprisingly firm *against all the
odds* and it is this which in Israel's eyes stamps him as her
'successful' hero, though few scholars, if any, note the fact.

Unlike Coats, T. L. Thompson is willing to recognise the biblical writer's *unheroic* portrait of Moses. However, he too is just as blind to the god-of-the-marginals ideology. He suggests that Moses is purposefully written down so that Yahweh can be written up. (*The Bible in History* Jonathan Cape 1999 p. 93) In doing so he pulls off the incredible feat of trivialising not just Moses and Yahweh but also the Yahwist and the Bible itself! I find it amazing anyone can fail to recognise that Moses *and Yahweh as his ideology* are central to this story, making it preposterous to suggest that Moses is written down.

Conclusion

All the evidence suggests Coats is justified in saying these texts portray Moses as the hero. However, given the all too numerous unheroic aspects of the portrait, which cannot be excised without robbing the story of its essential character, it cannot possibly be an *apolitical folk hero* we are speaking about. Clearly, Moses acts as the heroic servant of the ideological god of the marginals, and not as the servant of any religious god, whether conservative or liberal.

7

The Baby Girl Abandoned at Birth
(Ezekial 16)

The Transcendent Stranger-God:
A Revisionist Masterpiece

An Ideological Revision of Exodus 3

There are two hugely influential revisionist stories in the Old Testament. The first is Genesis 1 which, as we have seen, is positioned in order to control the way in which people go on to read (i.e. misread) the revolutionary stories that follow it. The second is this story in Ezekiel which is designed to control, if rather less obviously, the way in which we now read (misread) the equally important, revolutionary Exodus stories. I say 'less obviously' because Ezekiel 16 was never slotted in before Exodus 3 so as to make its objective clear. But how does Ezekiel 16 seek to control Exodus 3? Well, it's very subtle indeed. And because we were required to cover so much ground when looking at Moses' overall strategy in the previous Study, I hope you will permit me a moment now to re-examine Exodus 3 specifically. This will enable us to properly understand what Ezekiel was up to.

Exodus 3: The Birth of the Marginal Ideology

As we have seen the story of the burning bush is a true revolutionary Hebrew text and as pivotal a piece of writing as can be found anywhere in the Bible. It describes how Yahweh revealed himself to Moses *as the god of the marginals* and how he explained to Moses what he had to do to bring about the Hebrews' liberation. How can I be certain this was what the writer had in mind? The answer is straightforward, for he actually has Yahweh describe himself as 'the god of the marginals' when he instructs

73

Moses what to say when taking his people's case to Pharaoh:

> Then you and the elders are to go to the king of Egypt and say
> to him, "The LORD, the God of the Hebrews, has met with
> us ..." (Genesis 3:18)

This is simply a repetition of what he had previously told Moses
to say on returning to *his own* people. Only then, for obvious
reasons, he did not use the pejorative, official term 'Hebrew =
Marginal' but rather the more familiar 'God of Your Fathers':

> Go, assemble the elders of Israel and say to them, "The LORD,
> the God of your fathers—the God of Abraham, Isaac and
> Jacob—appeared to me and said: ..." (Genesis 3:15)

So there really can be no doubt about it. In Exodus 3 the author is
explicitly making the point that Yahweh is the Hebrew's god ...
the god who represents their outlook and interests as rubbished
marginals. This means that what we have here in this text is not,
as has usually been supposed, an extraordinary *religious*
pronouncement containing some private revelation of privileged
information concerning 'the true nature of God'. Rather it is a
quite ordinary *ideological* pronouncement such as might be
expected from any god who represented the interests of an
identifiable group of people in the ancient Near East. The only
thing which marks this text out as special is the fact that Yahweh
does not claim to represent some respectable civilisation-group
but, on the contrary, civilisation's most miserable and despised
outcasts.

The Burning Bush: Symbol of the Marginals' Partnership God

This story about a burning bush sounds very strange and magical
to our modern ears. However, ancient people would immediately

have understood that the writer was simply using the normal mythological vocabulary (symbolism) of the day to describe how Moses, as an exiled political leader, worked out a strategy to defend the perspective and interests of his marginal/Hebrew people. For them, therefore, there would have been nothing more complicated or superstitious to extrapolate than that.

We know the focus of the story is this bush that is on fire but which is not consumed. There can be no doubt that the writer is making a significant point in using this striking symbol, but how is it to be understood? Well, as we have seen, in your normal (i.e. conservative) Semitic culture it was said to be dangerous to approach too near to a god, for you risked being consumed by his autocratic power. Because of this it was deemed necessary that centrarchical officers (a hierarchy of priests headed by the king himself) should be appointed to act as *intermediaries*. Needless to say, we are not talking about what actually was experienced as happening. People did not as a matter of fact spontaneously combust. *All we are dealing with is a powerful symbolic expression of your normal centrarchical ideology.* Here in our story of the burning bush, on the other hand, because we are dealing with the worldview of an abnormal group of trashed marginals we have the complete opposite. Instead of Yahweh being a normal, authoritarian god who represents an authoritarian ideology, what we have is Yahweh as a marginal god who represents a non-authoritarian, marginal ideology. This means that instead of 'naturally' consuming, Yahweh is said to 'unnaturally' abide in an intimate, on-the-level, relationship with his people: a situation later wonderfully described as a covenant agreement. If that does not constitute the perfect symbol for representing the marginal ideology then I don't know what does!

The Marginals' Reactive Strategy

However, this is not all, for the rest of the chapter goes on to describe the equally unusual marginal *strategy* which accompanied this most unusual marginal *ideology*. Most political strategies are *proactive* and involve differing ways of bringing *coercive pressure* to bear on a given situation whether through argument, organisation, civil disobedience and unrest, or outright violence. Though we tend to downplay them as ineffective, there do exist, however, alternative *reactive* strategies which consist of trying to get people to alter their behaviour voluntarily by publicly exposing the iniquitous way in which they treat others and so *shaming* them into changing their ways. Such strategies are called reactive because, rather than attempting to force people to change, they work simply by throwing light on situations, leaving others free to react as they will. Though it is undoubtedly true that reactive strategies have a far less immediate and brutal effect on a situation, it has to be said that when they do work *the effect is fundamentally more lasting* since the change is brought about voluntarily and so, to that extent, is real.

A further point worth bearing in mind is that, though all classes within society habitually struggle amongst themselves using proactive strategies of various kinds, marginals, as social failures, have no capacity for proactive endeavour. They have no choice in the matter when it comes to changing the world; shaming being their only viable option. Reactivity, it would seem, is the strategy of the weak and, as such, is naturally despised by the strong. That said, it is clearly the strategy we see employed in Exodus 3: Yahweh tells Moses to return to Egypt and go to the authorities with the request that the Hebrews be allowed to leave. Given that, as marginals, the Hebrews have no coercive power it stands to reason that Moses is going to have to shame the Egyptians into letting the Hebrews go. This explains his enormous reluctance and the argument which ensues between him and God in which all the difficulties and drawbacks are examined. Some will argue Yahweh provided Moses with a bit of heavenly magic to make up for the Hebrews' lack of coercive power but this is to misread the texts. The plagues as signs and wonders are simply the writer's way of saying that because of the amazing creative power and clarity of their ideology, the Hebrews invariably won the argument in their debates with the Egyptian authorities; the only problem being that this tended to harden Pharaoh's heart rather than soften it. In other words you have to understand that this heavenly magic too was reactive not proactive. As we have seen, the situation as we have it at present in the Bible is not very clear but this is only because the text has been doctored by revisionist editors who wished to get rid of what they would have seen as the week-kneed god of the marginals, so as to replace him with their own, more robust religious and transcendent, conservative God.

The Baby Girl story as a rewrite of Exodus

So, now we come to Ezekiel and what he was doing when, sometime later, he offered his own take on the proceedings. But what makes me think that the story of the baby girl abandoned at birth is Ezekiel's retelling of this story of the burning bush? Well, just reading the first few sentences should be enough to convince:

This is what the Sovereign LORD says to Jerusalem: "Your ancestry and birth were in the land of the Canaanites; your father was an Amorite and your mother a Hittite. On the day you were born your cord was not cut, nor were you washed with water to make you clean, nor were you rubbed with salt or wrapped in cloths. No one looked on you with pity or had compassion enough to do any of these things for you. Rather, you were thrown out into the open field, for on the day you were born you were despised. Then I passed by and saw you kicking about in your blood, and as you lay there in your blood I said to you, 'Live!' I made you grow like a plant of the field. You grew up and developed and became the most beautiful of jewels. Your breasts were formed and your hair grew, you who were naked and bare. Later I passed by, and when I looked at you and saw that you were old enough for love, I spread the corner of my garment over you and covered your nakedness. I gave you my solemn oath and entered into a covenant with you, declares the Sovereign LORD, and you became mine. ..." (Ezekiel 16:3-8)

OK, so it's clear, isn't it, that Ezekiel is here giving us his own account of Israel's origins but, apart from the obvious story form, in what significant way does he alter what we find in the Exodus text? Well, before I unmask it as the revisionist plot it is let me first take my hat off to it as a truly remarkable work. Though ideologically dubious in the extreme it is undoubtedly a great and wonderfully powerful piece of writing.

The Marginals' God becomes a Stranger God

Ezekiel manages to transform the Exodus story from a magnificent revolutionary marginal text into a blinding piece of conservative, religious writing by subtly altering the relationship between Yahweh and Israel. In Exodus 3, the relationship is between the god of the marginals and his people. Here, in Ezekiel's story of the baby girl abandoned at birth, the relationship is between a marginal Israel and a *stranger* god who happens to have pity on her and so who *chooses* to help her. At first sight you might think such a change is comparatively insignificant but therein lies Ezekiel's subtlety for, as was the case with Genesis 1, you are not supposed to see what is happening before your very eyes. If Ezekiel had not drawn such an impressively powerful picture of Israel as a helpless marginal community you would never have bought his wretched tableau. But, precisely because he performs such a great job you drop your guard and end up paying way over the score for a worthless bit of junk. For what you don't notice is that by a sleight of hand he has removed Yahweh as the ideologically disturbing god of the marginals and replaced him with the infinitely less disturbing conservative alternative: Yahweh, the merciful and condescending, religious transcendent God. But if you happen to like conservative religion as many do, why should you bother about Ezekiel's duplicity? Well, the fact is that conservative religion is expressly designed to get you to close your eyes to reality and take authority on trust. This, of course, is a recipe for disaster. Marginal ideology, on the other hand, is intentionally designed to get you to open your eyes to what is going on; a condition that is generally helpful even if you don't, as is often the case, like what you see.

Sad Proof that Ezekiel's Undermining Strategy Worked

Perhaps you will be saying to yourself that this business of controlling Exodus 3 is a very unlikely story but let me read to you what Walter Brueggemann, one of the foremost Old Testament scholars of our day, has to say about Exodus 3:

> When it first cried out in pain, Israel addressed no one and did not know its cry would be heard. Israel cried because it had to, but it knew of no one to address. The hurt of Israel, however, does not float in an unreceptive space. It is heard by none other than Yahweh, who becomes in the moment of hearing the God of Israel. This God, alone in the world of the gods, is like a magnet that attracts and draws hurt to God's own self. ...Yahweh is now implicated irreversibly in Israel's hurt. God is bonded to Israel around the quintessential human reality of hurt. The God of Israel will never again be unhurt or unaware of Israel's hurt. God takes the hurt of earth into God's own life and heaven is thereby transformed. The hurt, noticed and voiced, becomes the peculiar mode of linking earth to heaven, Israel to Yahweh. ... In obedience to Israel's cry of hurt, God acts, intervening not only to cherish

the hurting ones, not only to stand in solidarity, but also to act in power against those who initiate, sponsor, and perpetuate the hurt. The voiced hurt of Israel is the material base from which the holy power of God is activated to transform, destabilize, and reorder the world. (Brueggemann, *Old Testament Theology* Fortress Press 1992, pp.46-7)

Once again I think you will agree this is wonderful stuff which shows every sign that it has come directly from Ezekiel 16 but I put it to you it has nothing, manifestly nothing, to do with what we find in Exodus 3 ... or so it seems to me. I decided to take the matter up directly with Walter Brueggemann, writing to him thus:

Perhaps you will permit me just one more question before I close. I know you are probably a very busy man but I have to exploit my luck in holding your attention while it lasts! It's about your idea that in the Exodus texts Yahweh is presented as a stranger God who just happens to be attentive to a cry of distress. You will understand that this is a crucial issue for me for if you are right then I must be wrong, my position being entirely based on the understanding that in Exodus Yahweh is presented as the god of the Hebrew marginals. Of course I must concede from the start that in Ezekiel's *retelling* of the story (in Chapter 16) the position is quite clear and that here Yahweh is without doubt the passing stranger who *chooses* to have pity on Israel. So we both have to presume this was the way the Exodus story *tended to be understood at the time when the tradition was being formalised.* But was that the way it was meant to be understood in the beginning? With all of this in mind I would like to ask how you account for the expression 'The God of your fathers' in Exodus 3:6,13,15 and the expression 'The Lord God of the Hebrews' in Exodus 3:18? Do they not constitute strong evidence against your 'stranger' thesis?

Here then is how Professor Brueggemann cryptically, though politely, replied:

> I think 'God of the Hebrews' is exactly for strangers. The one about 'the fathers' I think is an attempt to link to Genesis. I would not force that reading, but that is how it looks to me.

I don't know how you understand what is being said here but I find it an evasion and I fancy that, in heaven, it brought out a smile on Ezekiel's face.

8

Job

The Transcendent God Unmasked as a Conservative Lie

The Story as a Mess

This is a complicated study. It is not just the amount of background information you need in order to be able to make head or tail of what is going on. It's also the fact that it requires a steady nerve and concentration in order to succeed in untangling the editorial mess that has been bequeathed to us.

The Outline of the Book

You may find it strange that I talk about the book as an editorial mess since on the surface it appears well planned. It consists of a short prologue (Chapters 1 and 2) and an even shorter epilogue (Chapter 42:7-14) both written in prose. These sandwich the main body of the work which is a long debate written in poetry and which consists of three cycles of speeches between Job and his friends Eliphaz, Bildad and Zophar.

Problems Due to a Major Dislocation

However, appearances can be deceptive for, as we will soon find, nothing in the book of Job is quite what it seems. The prologue shows clearly that Job's many sufferings are due to the fact that God has permitted Satan[14] to put the righteous man Job to the test. But what is surprising is that neither Satan himself nor what he is up to is ever alluded to in the long debate that follows, even though the question of human suffering and the reason for it is discussed by everyone except Job, at some length. That said, the idea of Israel as the 'righteous servant of Yahweh' who is 'proved' in some way by suffering does have echoes elsewhere in the Bible (notably in the servant songs in Isaiah) and the idea certainly became central in later Rabbinic literature, as the following delightful parable shows:

> 'The Lord trieth the righteous' (Ps 11.5) Rabbi Jose ben Hanina (3rd c C.E.) said: 'When the flax worker knows that his flax is good, he keeps on beating it, and it grows better; he keeps on beating it and it acquires more body. But when he knows that his flax is bad he scarcely beats it at all, and then it bursts. Even so does the Holy One, blessed be He, not try the wicked, but only the righteous.'
> (Asher Feldman, *The Parables and Similies of the Rabbis* Cambridge University Press 1924, pp.61-2)

However, none of this 'maturation' or 'proving-through-suffering' business appears in the great debate involving Job, nor does it figure in Yahweh's subsequent response out of the whirlwind, for that matter. This means we have a major unexplained dislocation to deal with between the body of the work and its presumed editorial setting.

A Young Man and More Problems Still

But that is just for starters. You see, whereas the first two cycles in the debate are fairly straightforward, if to our modern minds somewhat repetitive, the third cycle is very strange. For not only is Bildad's contribution this time round rather short, as if he was running out of steam, but Zophar's participation is completely missing. Instead, we have a long contribution by a young man named Elihu (Chapters 32-37) who appears out of the blue as a newcomer to the debate. He takes issue not just with Job but also with Job's three friends. This presumably means we must take it he was present all the time even though neither the prologue, nor the debate itself, nor indeed the epilogue where Job is cleared and his friends condemned, recognises his presence in any way, shape or form. That said, it cannot be denied that this young man introduces a significant and welcome new focus to the debate. Previously the three friends had pitilessly argued that since God is sovereign, righteous and gracious, Job must have committed some heinous secret sin to have been visited by such terrible misfortune. On the other hand, what is significant about Elihu's contribution is that whereas the three friends are clearly guilty of disgracefully demanding Job should repent of a secret sin he never committed but which they themselves have simply invented for their own dubious purposes, Elihu argues that Job is most certainly guilty of a very different, though equally terrible, offence: arrogantly daring to question God's justice and, what is more, having the brass neck to express a desire to have his day in court where he can make his case to God *in person*.

Another Major Dislocation Involving the Purpose of the Book

All the signs are that this speech by the young Elihu was added by some later editor. However, you can't deny it serves an important purpose in the book as it is now stands since it carefully prepares the reader for what immediately follows; namely Yahweh's personal appearance and big speech. The fact that such a preparation was deemed necessary draws attention to a second dislocation which has to do with the actual purpose of the book itself. You see, if all we had to go on were the introductory and epilogue prose sections we would naturally conclude the subject matter of the work is how to square innocent suffering with a God who is sovereign, righteous and gracious. Seen in this light, the answer the book appears to give is that such suffering, though admittedly uncomfortable, is temporary and constitutes a necessary stage that has to be endured and worked through if one is to arrive at the much higher state of happiness and blessedness on the other side. The trouble with this general scenario, so well reflected in the flax parable above, is that though it can be made to square to a certain extent with the debate between Job and his friends (the debate itself being seen as all part and parcel of the ordeal Job has to endure) it in no way fits with what comes next: the whirlwind episode where Yahweh defies all expectation and grants Job's outrageous demand by meeting him face to face in court. Indeed, if we take it that the book's general message is that suffering should be seen as 'a trying passage to a higher state' wouldn't you agree that it would have been far better to have this great debate between Job and his friends function simply as a prelude to a story which then went on to show how Job benefited from his terrible ordeal, turning it in later life to his great advantage ... as indeed the epilogue would seem to suggest had been the case? But that is emphatically not what the story seems to be getting at in this new debate between Job and Yahweh. In fact, at this point the whole purpose of the book is thrown into doubt since Yahweh's dramatic appearance strongly suggests a completely different issue is at stake; one which has to do with the vindication of Job's stance rather than a rationalisation of his suffering.

Yahweh's Big Speech as the Focus of the Story

So how can we make sense of Yahweh's big speech, which must have been the focal point of the original work since it still stands artistically as the climax of the disjointed and rather confusing text we have on our plate? Well, Elihu's intervention must surely be a first step in working out how things originally stood. It firmly drags our attention away from this whole 'justification of innocent suffering' on which the prologue and epilogue has wrongly caused us to become fixated and brings us back to where we should surely have been all along: Job's outrageous cheek in demanding a personal confrontation with Yahweh and the whirlwind speech itself, as Yahweh's response. The only drawback as regards this 'step in the right direction' is the fact that Elihu's intervention is never justified or for that matter condemned by what happens later.

Sorting Out the Mess

Job's 'Friends' as Typical Status Quo Conservatives

OK. So you see something of the tangled mess we find ourselves in? Let's try now to sort it out. To start with we need to nail down the political viewpoint of Job's comforters since it would make sense to assume that it is their ideological position that the original work was attacking. To do this we have to analyse what was their view of God. The thing that characterises the 'God' whom Job's friends refer to in their speeches is his transcendence: his all-powerful, far removed and hence essentially unknowable nature. Now, it is important to understand that scholars tend these days to speak about a defining intellectual crisis which arose all over the ancient world during the first millennium BCE. This supposedly came about as a result of the growth of great empires, which gave rise to an awareness of the out-dated irrelevance of the old local traditional gods. Scholars see this crisis as having been resolved in different ways in different parts of the region. In the Aegean, the gods and the cosmology of Homer and Hesiod were rejected by the Greek playwrights in the fifth century BCE who ruthlessly exposed the popular fantasies about the gods. The old gods were also dismissed by Plato in the fourth century who portrayed the ideal philosopher as a servant of reflection and seeker after self-knowledge. In India the same intellectual crisis, in which the traditional gods with their feet of clay were confronted, resulted in the writings of Buddhism. However, elsewhere in Asia, somewhat in contrast to what happened in Greece, the traditions of the past were affirmed rather than rejected. They were seen as expressions of true though limited human perceptions of reality. This resulted in the defining concept of the transcendent high god found in the scriptures of both Zoroastrianism and the Bible, the unknowable and universal 'God of heaven' being Ahura Mazda for the Persians and Elohe Shamayim for the conquered nation of Israel.

Now I'm not suggesting you should simply take this analysis on trust since scholars are well known for changing their minds. However, I would suggest that it makes it clear enough that this notion of the transcendent high god was an empire construct and hence a deeply *status quo* and conservative idea. For isn't its objective to teach people to accept established authority without question, believing that those in the higher realms responsible for making decisions, whoever they are, not only know what they are doing but also clearly operate for the best even though this may not necessarily seem obvious to those living humbly on the ground?

The Original Book of Job as a Revolutionary Work

Given the conservative *status quo* position of Job's adversaries it stands to reason that the book of Job must originally have been written specifically as an anti-*status quo* or revolutionary work in which the objective was to discredit this conservative stance which Job's friends, one and all, embody. This means that lying somewhere behind all the revisionist editor's conservative gloss (in which the work is supposedly all about suffering as a way to a higher state of blessedness) we should expect to find in the conduct of Job a revolutionary performance which seeks to expose and shame the conservative attitude of his detractors[15].

Job: a Suffering Individual or a Personification of Faithful Israel?

In all honesty I am bound to admit that I have a problem here. You see, the Bible's revolutionary talk of shaming, which is well authenticated in scripture, is clearly a political strategy in which the objective is for Israel, as the faithful servant of Yahweh, to change the way in which the world (notably the Gentile world) behaves. She is to do this by putting on a collective demonstration of radical solidarity: loving the neighbour as the self.

However, what we have here in the story of Job does not at first sight appear to be an account of a collective display of solidarity but rather a description of one man's suffering as a result of incredible misfortune. It is true, of course, that there are many stories in the Old Testament which see individuals as standing collectively for groups of people and in many cases the group in question turns out to be Israel. So there is nothing intrinsically difficult in seeing the righteous man Job as a personification of Yahweh's faithful servant: the true Israel. That is easy. What is more difficult, though, is seeing Job's sufferings as a depiction of the afflictions which Israel was forced to endure as a result of her faithfulness. For Job's sufferings, at least as they are depicted in the prologue, have every appearance of being entirely accidental: the consequence of what we would today call bad luck[16]. In the dialogues themselves, of course, it is much less clear precisely why Job suffers and it seems to me that it could perfectly well be understood that he suffers not because of accidental misfortune but rather because his life's enterprise ... whatever this may be ... has apparently proved to be unsuccessful, not to say counter-productive.

Revolutionary Prophets and Conservative Priests in Post Exilic Judah

Of course, if we knew the circumstances under which the author of the original piece was working, we might be in a better position to judge whether he meant Job's misfortune to be under-stood as resulting from individual misfortune (as the biblical editors clearly wished readers to think[17]) or alternatively from some kind of political failure. The question is, can we work this out? Well, the book of Job is taken by most scholars to be a late post-exilic work. This means that it was most probably written towards the end of a time of fierce ideological struggle between two important groups within the semi-autonomous Judean community established by the Persians in what is known as the post-exilic period. One party involved in this struggle was a revolutionary prophetic-group. They saw themselves as the disciples of Second Isaiah and you can find their political tracts in Isaiah 56-66 and Zecheriah 9-14. The opposing party consisted of a conservative priestly-group. They saw themselves as the followers of Ezekiel (for my money a died-in-the-wool conservative revisionist) and you can find their political tracts in the books of Haggai and Zecheriah 1-8. Sadly, it was the conservative priestly-group which won the day, if not the ideological argument. It took control of the community and this meant that the prophetic-group was progressively excluded from influence, its arguments becoming increasingly shrill and desperate as time went on until finally it was silenced. Given this scenario, it is not difficult to see Job as the embodiment of this squeezed and marginalised, revolutionary prophetic-group and to see his deeply conservative friends as the embodiment of the new conservative establishment.

Job: the Personification of the Revolutionary Prophetic Group?

If you try and exclude from your thoughts everything that is to be found in the prologue and epilogue, including the almost universally accepted notion that the book is about the problem of evil, you will find it surprisingly easy to read the dialogues between Job and his friends as the embodiment of this post-exilic ideological struggle. Job, standing for the revolutionary prophetic-group, sees himself as Yahweh's true servant whose task it is to shame the Gentile world by putting on a display of radical solidarity: loving the neighbour as the self[18]. However, his experience is that instead of bringing in the Kingdom, this performance of 'marginal righteousness', which he says he has exercised all his life with the utmost care and attention, has simply meant that he has increasingly become a pariah within the community itself. How can this be since Yahweh's promise is that if Israel does her job Yahweh will vindicate her efforts? Not only does this not happen, apparently proving to all the world that his project must be wrong-headed, but worse still, he is forced to endure the strictures of his establishment-friends who tell him that if he has failed it can only be because he 'personally' is at fault since the fault cannot conceivably lie with Yahweh! Of course, Job never ceases to protest that this is not the case but since God does not vindicate his efforts he is left without an argument and has to endure not just his 'group' failure but also the triumph and smug hypocritical self-satisfaction of his political opponents. Understandably, he wishes that Yahweh would simply blot him out. He could, of course, curse Yahweh and die but this he steadfastly refuses to do. Instead, he demands that if he will not vindicate his efforts then Yahweh should at least be prepared to meet him and give him the satisfaction of knowing why this promised vindication has been withheld.

Job the Personification as an Alternative Reading

In this reading of the text (and let me state very plainly that it is simply an alternative reading which in no way requires that the text should be changed) it is at once crystal clear why the climax of the work has to be Yahweh's personal appearance. For in this 'new' reading everything hinges on the vindication of Yahweh's righteous servant ...

> I know that my redeemer lives,
> and that in the end he will stand on the earth.
> And after my skin has been destroyed,
> yet in my flesh I will see God;
> I myself will see him
> with my own eyes—I, and not another. (Job 19:25-27)

... and that is precisely what Yahweh's personal appearance

achieves. This vindication is absolutely central to all revolutionary Hebrew thinking since the Hebrew revolution itself depended on it. The contract was that the Hebrew community had to stand up for itself and present the world with a perfect demonstration of what it meant to live together in radical solidarity, loving the neighbour as the self, while Yahweh had to vindicate this effort by seeing to it that the demonstration worked by shaming the world to its senses. Of course, if the demonstration did not work ... because for some reason Yahweh stayed his hand ... then the Hebrew revolutionaries naturally became in Paul's telling words 'of all men most miserable'[19]. This is precisely what Job complains has happened to him. He is not beset with accidental misfortune, as readers of the Bible automatically (though quite wrongly) suppose because of the biblical editors' machinations. He is beside himself with anguish because he had done his best to perform his side of the covenant bargain yet apparently Yahweh has failed to fulfil his promise and do his bit. As a result Job has to endure not simply the pain of being a common failure but rather the pain of being a monumental one... not merely in the eyes of the whole world but in the eyes of his bitter ideological opponents: the conservative, revisionist hypocrites. No wonder he is angry ... angry enough to curse the day that he was born ... though not angry enough to curse God and die.

Face-to-Face Encounter as Vindication of the Alternative Reading

However, it's not simply that this revolutionary reading squares admirably well with the text, making excellent sense of it; unlike the Biblical editors' revisionist religious reading which not only fits very badly but also turns the text into religious nonsense. It also proves itself to be the correct reading, beyond any shadow of doubt, when Yahweh meets Job *face to face* (Job 42.5). Why do I say this? Well, in conservative Semitic literature the norm is that for a human-being a face-to-face encounter with a god spells instant death. This deeply conservative idea was of immense political importance in justifying the centrarchical structures which, so it was pretended, served to mediate between deity and people. As we have seen, Moses' vision of the desert bush that appeared to be on fire but which did not burn (Exodus 3:1-3) was a direct contradiction of this pernicious conservative notion. It established the fundamental revolutionary principle that Yahweh, as the god of the marginals, required no mediation; the relationship between him and his faithful people being a 'personal' contract between equal unequals with obligations on both sides. Of course, according to the tradition, Israel was seldom if ever faithful but when she was, as in the person of Moses himself, this face to face relationship is unequivocally confirmed:

> The LORD would speak to Moses face to face, as one speaks to a friend. (Exodus 33:11)

This classic position is twice reaffirmed in the Jacob and Esau story. First, when through an all-night struggle Jacob at last manages finally to become Yahweh's equal-unequal, covenant partner and so the personification of faithful Israel:

> Then the man said, "Your name will no longer be Jacob, but Israel, because you have struggled with God and with humans and have overcome." Jacob said, "Please tell me your name." But he replied, "Why do you ask my name?" Then he blessed him there. So Jacob called the place Peniel, saying, "It is because I saw God face to face, and yet my life was spared." (Genesis 32:28-30)

and then again when the now faithful Jacob realises to his aston-ishment that his invidiously competitive relationship with his brother Esau has miraculously changed:

> "No, please!" said Jacob. "If I have found favour in your eyes, accept this gift from me. For to see your face is like seeing the face of God, now that you have received me favourably. Please accept the present that was brought to you, for God has been gracious to me and I have all I need." And because Jacob insisted, Esau accepted it. (Genesis 33:10-11)

We get echoes of this same classic situation in the story of Elijah who too had a struggle in becoming the god of the marginals' faithful servant. At first in his battles with Ahab and Jezebel he had behaved as a blood-thirsty revolutionary. However, forced to flee into the desert he had time to reflect on the errors of his ways so that he was ready to understand when Yahweh finally instructed him to go to the mountain of God for his face-to-face encounter:

> The LORD said, "Go out and stand on the mountain in the presence of the LORD, for the LORD is about to pass by." Then a great and powerful wind tore the mountains apart and shattered the rocks before the LORD, but the LORD was not in the wind. After the wind there was an earthquake, but the LORD was not in the earthquake. After the earthquake came a fire, but the LORD was not in the fire. And after the fire came a gentle whisper. When Elijah heard it, he pulled his cloak over his face and went out and stood at the mouth of the cave. (1 Kings 19:11-13)

In short what we have in all of this is the classic portrait of faithful Israel in two distinct domains. First, an 'historical' domain where Israel's two great prophets, Moses and Elijah, are portrayed as meeting Yahweh face to face. Then, second, in a 'story' or 'representational' domain where Jacob, as a personification, is described as becoming faithful Israel and thus seeing Yahweh face to face.

Does not all of this suggest that in the story of Job we have, once again, this classic portrait of faithful Israel as the one who, *altogether extraordinarily,* sees Yahweh face to face? Of course, Job is put forward as a 'representation' and not an 'historical character' since, unlike Moses and Elijah, there is no significant talk about Job elsewhere in the Bible. This means that we are surely right in seeing Job as the personification of the prophetic revolutionary group in Post exilic Judah[20].

Post Script

Undoubtedly people will complain that in my analysis of the book I have done everything I possibly can to avoid seeing what it is all too obviously talking about: how God graciously conde-scends to meet in person those who undeservedly suffer, as so many people unfortunately do even today. However, I totally reject such a criticism since I am more than happy to accept that the revisionist biblical editors did indeed wish to produce such a comforting religious reading, as one can tell from the way in which they have carefully crafted it out of a pre-existing revolu-tionary political text. My only concern is to point out that such a reading cannot possibly have been the way in which the original writer wrote this work. For the crucial parts of the story, which is to say Job's passionate plea to be personally heard by Yahweh and Yahweh's response out of the whirlwind, cannot be made to fit with a religious understanding without trivialising the story. It may or may not be the case that God condescends to 'visit' individual sufferers as religious people like to maintain but there is simply no use in pretending that the Bible is talking about such matters since it is only in the most exceptional circumstances that it describes face-to-face encounters with Yahweh. Since my personal interest is with the political ideas of the original revolutionary writer rather than with the conservative religious gloss which the revisionist editors have invented to cover these up, I leave it to others to expand on the religious trivialisation with which the biblical editors have left us.

9

Jonah and the Whale (Jonah 1–4)

Lampooning the Revisionists

History or Spoof?

Everyone knows the story of Jonah and the whale, the only question on peoples' minds being; is it true? So I suppose this is where we will have to begin, even though it pains me to have to do so. For let's face it, if we are asking ourselves such a question we shouldn't really be reading this story or indeed anything else in the Bible since the basic requisite for reading the Bible is that we have our sharpest wits about us. This is the story of a man who is swallowed by a whale and who spends three days in its stomach before being vomited out. That in itself should be more, much more, than enough to tell us it never happened. But did the writer wish his readers to believe it happened? Everything indicates he did not ...

The Biblical Editors' Conservative Reading of the Story as History

However, before crediting the writer with a modicum of sense, let's amuse ourselves for a moment by reading his story as if it was meant to be understood as something miraculous which actually happened, as the Biblical editors wanted readers to do. If we do this then what is the point we find it making? Well, following the lines of the priestly writer of Genesis 1, I suppose we would have to read it as if it was about obeying God. Doing this would account well for the first half of the story. In this, God orders Jonah to do something for him but, not fancying the job, Jonah refuses and tries to escape, only for God to catch up with him and punish him for being disobedient. Then, after a suitable period of chastisement, Jonah abjectly repents, whereupon God relents and offers him forgiveness.

Now had the story ended there I would have been obliged to admit it makes reasonable, if at the same time rather dull and authoritarian religious sense. But the story does not end there. As we shall see, after initially dragging his heels, Jonah does eventually dutifully carry out God's instructions that he preach repentance to the people of Nineveh. However, he becomes incredibly grumpy when God crowns his efforts with success ... a grumpiness that is made even worse when God tries to pull him out of his bad mood by playing a game on him with a super-fast-growing plant! From an authoritarian point of view none of this makes any sense so we are faced with the fact that if this story was meant to be read in an authoritarian religious manner, as an account of something miraculous that actually happened, it's a third rate offering in every department which is embarrassing if it turns out to be true. This, of course, is the reason why preachers who offer a miraculous/authoritarian reading of the text only ever deal with the first half of the story.

A Sensible Reading of the Story as a Revolutionary Spoof

But the story was never meant to be to be read in this ridiculous fashion. For it is not just a story in which a man tells his shipmates to throw him overboard whereupon he is immediately swallowed by a whale; it is also a story in which a city is so big that it takes three days to travel to its centre and a story in which a vine can, in one night, grow so big as to provide an arbour under which one can sit in its shade! So if you don't now get the point that the story is a spoof you never will, for nothing I can possibly say about it will prove half as convincing as what the story itself says!

Taking it as read then that the story is a spoof (and a magnificent one at that) what is it trying to say ... not to us ... but to the people for whom it was written? Well, given that it is not a revisionist piece of conservative religious writing, it must be a genuine, revolutionary Hebrew offering since that is the only real alternative. Furthermore, although the story is ostensibly about an Israelite prophet named Jonah, son of Amittai, whom we know, from 2 Kings 14:25, lived during the Assyrian period, scholars are uniformly convinced it was, in fact, written in the later post-exilic period. I would agree with this judgement for two reasons. First is the curious fact that Jonah speaks of himself as a Hebrew, using the word not in its original sense in which it meant an unwashed and unloved marginal, but rather in its late sense when the word had lost its pejorative connotation and simply meant a *bona fide* Israelite. This is an important point to make, for the Jonah of this story is, in fact, a died-in-the-wool revisionist and anything but a revolutionary marginal. *What is more, he is clearly the butt of the story and not its hero.* The second reason why I would judge the story to be late and post-exilic is the fact that I see it as taking for granted that Israel's revolutionary job is to be the light to lighten the Gentiles. This means that it must have been written some time after Second Isaiah had put this revolutionary principle on the map.

A Devastating Attack on Israel's Inward-Looking Conservative Nationalism

For my part I see the writer's objective as being to question the inward-looking and nationalistic ideas which the priestly hierocrats had established in the post-exilic community. These revisionists were no longer concerned to be part of Yahweh's revolutionary world-transforming scheme (in which Israel's job was to put on such a successful demonstration of what it meant to be a community living together in radical solidarity that the Gentile world would come and ask her how it was done so they could do it themselves). As religious conservatives, the revisionists had become 'little' Israelites with eyes only for their own community. They believed that, using Ezekiel's blueprint for the new society, all they had to do was follow this to the letter, leaving Yahweh to magically do the rest.

So, the writer of our story cleverly sets up these revisionists in the tight-arsed Jonah, his figure of fun. With wicked irony in Chapter 1 he has Yahweh send down the command that Jonah must go as his prophet to the Gentile arch-enemy of the day, Assyria, and preach against it, denouncing its wickedness. To post-exilic revisionists this was fundamentally unfair, for two basic reasons. First, as they saw things it was Yahweh's job, not Israel's, to deal with the Gentiles, so Yahweh had no business to issue such a command. Second, since for them an Israelite's duty was simply to obey, there was no way in which Jonah, as an obedient revisionist, could refuse, even though the command itself was, to his way of thinking, entirely unwarranted. Beginning now to enjoy his own story, the writer describes Jonah as vainly seeking to escape Yahweh. However, being a pious man Jonah knows there is no way of doing this. So when a storm hits the boat in which he is endeavouring to flee, he quickly throws in the towel even before it is absolutely necessary, telling the sailors to save themselves by chucking him overboard. And so the story goes on with the writer enjoying every minute of it. When Jonah is eventually thrown into the sea, Yahweh saves him by having him swallowed by a conveniently placed whale! This then becomes the location in Chapter 2 for an extended prayer, just like the pious prayers you get in the Psalms in which conservative religious folk down through the ages, have always loved to wallow. I imagine the writer here splitting his sides, as indeed I do, in reading what he wrote.

Jonah Sees Yahweh as Being a Soft Lefty

And so to Chapter 3 in which Jonah is given a second chance. This is eye-catching in itself for 'a second chance' is precisely how Second Isaiah understands Cyrus's decree allowing the exiled Israelite leaders to return to Judah[21]. So now, with very bad grace, Jonah trudges off to Nineveh, enduring the extended three days travel needed to reach the civilisation world-centre of the day. There, as instructed, he preaches Yahweh's word against the Gentiles, doubtlessly hoping they will send him away with a flea in his ear just as the inhabitants of Sodom and Gomorrah had done to Lot when he had had the nerve to tell them off. That way Jonah will be able to enjoy the fun when Yahweh destroys the whole of Nineveh with brimstone and fire. Once again you can sense the writer's relish as he announces the big surprise that happened next ... something so unthinkable as to be beyond the wildest dreams even of a true Hebrew revolutionary: the whole population of Nineveh, to a man, repents in sackcloth and ashes!

Understandably, at this Jonah becomes quite beside himself with frustration and rage. He hadn't wanted to go to Nineveh in the first place since the Assyrians were Israel's most bitter enemies. He had expected Yahweh to defend Israel by destroying the Assyrians, as any pukka conservative god would have done but instead Yahweh had gone all soft and offered the Assyrians forgiveness if they repented ... and now they had! Jonah storms out of the city in a great pique and builds a cabin so that he can wait to see what God will now do.

Yahweh Puts Him Straight

Only here, at this late stage in the proceedings in Chapter 4, do we learn the story's true thrust. Yahweh now makes a concerted effort to try and get his wayward prophet to open his eyes and see what should always have been obvious to him: that He, Yahweh, the Lord of the Universe, has more on his mind than the petty concerns of little Israel who is simply his tool for bringing about world transformation. He does this by playing a little trick on Jonah. First he causes a vine to grow which affords Jonah some agreeable shade. Then, when Jonah is suitably comfortable, he suddenly causes it to die. Jonah, of course, is furious but Yahweh asks him to compare his own petty concern about the demise of the vine with the destruction of a vast city ... the outcome Jonah had at that very moment been willing to come about with such unthinking, righteous relish.

Pause

Looking Back at the Old Testament Stories and Forward to Jesus' Role.

Moving from the Old Testament to the New raises the question of the relationship between the Testaments themselves. Most people assume Jesus founded a new religion, Christianity; a new and improved form of Judaism. But this flies in the face of everything found in the texts. For the New Testament itself makes it unmistakably clear that Jesus' intention was rather to fulfil the Mosaic tradition, adding nothing to the Law and the Prophets. It explains he set about doing this by calling on his fellowcountrymen to join him in collectively performing as Yahweh's light; his objective being to demonstrate to the (Gentile) world what 'loving the neighbour as the self' consisted of. In doing this, his hope was that Yahweh would vindicate the exercise by bringing in his Kingdom, as he had always in the past promised he would do.

The New Testament writers claim, astonishingly enough, that Jesus actually succeeded in this aim even though everyone else at the critical moment deserted him. So, our purpose too is now clear: having forced our unwilling civilisational minds to grapple with what is involved in this revolutionary marginal exercise, we must proceed to judge for ourselves how successful Jesus was in putting it into effect. Then, when all is finished, we will finally be in a position to judge whether Yahweh did indeed stand by his promise, no religious magic of any description being involved in the exercise. But that, of course, is some way ahead!

Are you ready? Then let's continue!

10

The Parable of the Doctor (Mark 2:15-20)

Jesus Stakes His Ground as a Hebrew Revolutionary

Solidarity with Life's losers

Mark relates that in one of his first public acts, Jesus chose to demonstrate his revolutionary Hebrew (i.e. god-of-the-marginals) credentials by openly associating with publicans and sinners. This conduct scandalised morally upright folk who criticised him, though, apparently, only behind his back. When he heard about it, Jesus is said to have made a one-line parable rejoinder:

It is not the healthy who need a doctor, but the sick.

following this with another related remark:

I have not come to call the righteous, but sinners. (Mark 2:17)

Since it was righteous people who were criticising Jesus you might expect similar folk today to find Jesus' parable shocking but this is far from being the case. In fact, most people love it. For as a society we admire doctors, whom we see as men and women of standing within the community and eminently worthy of respect. Consequently, church-going folk are only too happy to see 'their man' Jesus describe himself as a doctor and therefore as someone who healed people not just of their physical ailments but of their spiritual and moral ailments as well. But is this what Jesus was in fact saying about himself?

There is no contesting that Jesus was using this parable to highlight some basic requirement regarding his own job. As I see it, he was saying that since his revolutionary business in performing as Yahweh's revealing light was designed to banish marginalisation from the community then, obviously, he couldn't avoid mixing with marginals themselves. However, there is plenty of evidence at hand to suggest that today's good people habitually use the 'doctor' feature in the story to read into the parable an establishment-minded, ideological colouring that Jesus never intended.

A Doctor as Someone of Standing in the Local Community

For example, people today often use the idea of Jesus speaking of himself as in some sense 'a doctor' to try and make out that, being a local man of some standing he must have countenanced social-standing itself. As we see things, to be a doctor is to be a professional working in a given locality, the job itself having status marking out the performer as a recognisable member of the local establishment. However, all the evidence suggests Jesus did not operate from a centre within a given locality, a fact which in itself is somewhat mindblowing. Indeed, he seems to have deliberately chosen to work in such a manner as to avoid the creation of a power-base and the only standing he acquired seems to have come purely by way of reputation. This means it had nothing to do with his membership of any earthly or, for that matter, heavenly establishment.

A Doctor as an Establishment Figure Who Speaks With Authority

Because being a doctor is not just a job this means that a doctor, by virtue of the fact of being a doctor, has a status. This gives the doctor authority over other people and turns him or her willy-nilly into a hierarchical or centrarchical figure. Consequently, it is hardly surprising that some people use this 'doctor' saying to suggest that Jesus saw himself in such a light. However, all the evidence suggests that Jesus was as much loath to speak down to people as he was to speak up to them. Everything we know about him shows that his practice was to speak all the time and to everyone strictly on-the-level. This does not mean that people did not see him as having authority. Clearly they did. However, it does mean that the authority they saw Jesus as possessing was not of the status kind (hierarchical or centrarchical) which people in those days associated with the scribes:

> When Jesus had finished saying these things, the crowds were amazed at his teaching, because he taught as one who had authority, and not as their teachers of the law. (Matthew 7:28-29)

It seems clear, therefore, that unlike the scribes' authority, Jesus' authority stemmed solely from the evident impact he made on people and this had nothing at all to do with his position within any earthly or, and I repeat, *heavenly* establishment.

A Doctor as Someone with Influence who Acts Proactively

There is another more subtle way in which people today manipulate this 'doctor' saying so as to breathe an untoward, authoritarian, ideological colouring into the biblical text. It has to do with the kind of strategy Jesus used. As I have already pointed out, most strategies are proactive, which makes it understandable (if not right) that scholars have almost universally argued that Jesus' strategy too was proactive. I have already underlined the important difference between proactive and reactive strategies and the aim of this book is to show that the Hebrew revolutionaries were the ones who actually invented the reactive strategy which aims to rid the world (civilisation) of marginalisation by demonstrating how to live, loving the neighbour as the self. I now want to take this one step further and say that what Jesus was doing was taking upon himself the job of bringing this Hebrew revolution to a head, thus fulfilling his own covenant obligation, by calling on all Israelites to join him in performing as 'Yahweh's light to lighten the Gentiles'. This, as you will probably know, is a phrase coined by Second Isaiah (another revolutionary Hebrew writer) to describe Israel's job as Yahweh's partner in transforming the world by the use of the Hebrew reactive strategy. If I am right, then it would naturally go without saying that Jesus would have been at pains to avoid telling people what to do from an assumed position of earthly or heavenly authority, after the manner of the scribes. The trouble is that nowadays we tend to see doctoring not as a reactive exercise but rather as a proactive endeavour *par excellence*. This means that Jesus' 'doctoring' parable now presents people with an unmissable opportunity to get rid of this weak-kneed reactive strategy which has always filled humanbeings, with the exception, of course, of marginals themselves, with contempt and disgust. So they proceed to colour the Gospel texts with their own vastly more acceptable authoritarian and proactive gloss, thus hiding from view the unacceptable truth which Jesus himself was at such pains to express!

A Strategy Never Even Mentioned by Twentieth Century Scholars

If you find all of this difficult to believe, as I am certain you will, I should tell you that I have examined the works of the foremost twentieth century 'historical Jesus' scholars (over fifty volumes written by thirty different authors[22]) and failed to find a single significant mention of Jesus' reactive, Isaianic strategy in them, so strong is our natural human desire *not to see* the truth that the Gospels themselves so clearly express.

The Unacceptable Nature of the Last being First

OK, I hear you say. So we misunderstand what Jesus meant by

doctoring but why should we find what he was actually saying shocking? Well, just look at Jesus' accompanying phrase:

I have not come to call the righteous, but sinners.(Mark 2:17)

This is surely unacceptable since Jesus appears to be privileging the wrong sort of people in calling upon the riff-raff *in priority* to seize the moment and join him in fulfilling Israel's destiny? This places the saying alongside a fair number of others which make very similar points by suggesting, for example, that tax gatherers and prostitutes *are the first* to get into the Kingdom. Some try to get rid of this prioritising aspect in Mark 2.17 by understanding Jesus as saying that people have to realise they are sinners before they can be saved. In other words, they try to make out that Jesus is simply saying here that he can't call the righteous because no such category exists and that people who consider themselves as righteous are not righteous at all but simply sinners who do not want to be saved. The trouble with this explanation is that it works by obscuring two crucial points. The first is the very real difference that exists between 'marginals' and 'civilisation-folk', here designated as 'sinners' and 'righteous'. The second is the fact that *Jesus seems to have been in the habit of constantly prioritising the wrong sort of people*. It seems to me that we civilisation-folk are prepared, at a pinch, to accept that room must be found for marginals since they too are made in God's image and, as is well known, God's graciousness and forgiveness know no bounds. However, the idea that such people are somehow better placed than we are, making it advisable for Jesus to prioritise their friendship in preference to ours, is simply appalling and cannot be true ... Yet clearly, very clearly, that is what Jesus was in the habit of both saying and doing! In this regard it's interesting to note that Luke himself was clearly shocked for he put in a rider so as to remove the sting:

Jesus answered them, 'It is not the healthy who need a doctor, but the sick. I have not come to call the righteous, but sinners *to repentance.'*(Luke 5:32)

What a cop out!

A Manifestly Reasonable Principle

From a god-of-the-marginals point of view all of this prioritising of life's losers makes perfect sense. It stands to reason the Hebrews were best placed, not because they were somehow better than the rest of us, which they weren't, but because, as marginals, they had the eyes to see what all of us are unable to perceive: the common flaw which is driving our civilisation to destruction. For their predicament made it all too obvious to them that every attempt to justify a privilege, in whatever shape or form, is just pure hypocrisy, *an hypocrisy we civilisation-folk conspire to keep closely under wraps.*

11

John the Baptist's Question (Matthew 11 and Luke 7)

John the Hebrew Revolutionary Who Got It Wrong

When John heard in prison what Christ was doing, he sent his disciples to ask him, "Are you the one who was to come, or should we expect someone else?" (Matthew 11:2)

A Criticism

Don't you think there's an implied criticism in this question which John sends to Jesus (a criticism which Jesus later rejects in talking about people like John as 'falling away' on account of him (see below))? And doesn't this seem surprising given the fact that John and Jesus are presented in the Gospel as allies? After all, Jesus was baptised by John and appears to have started off as one of John's disciples. So what point can John have been making in sending such a critical message from behind his prison wall?

Well, let's have a look at what we know about the story so far:

1) The Hebrew Revolutionary Endeavour

We know that throughout history, Israel's original revolutionary intent as a Hebrew (god-of-the-marginals) community had been to work together in a covenant partnership with Yahweh in order to shame the Gentile world into changing its oppressive ways. This was to be done by all true Israelites living together in radical solidarity, loving the neighbour as the self. Doing this would make it possible, when the time came, for Yahweh himself to bring in his Kingdom by actually softening the Gentiles' hearts.

2) The Conservative Revisionist Endeavour

As well as this, we know that, in time, this revolutionary intent had increasingly been undermined by those having power and authority within the community. The idea of these revisionists had been to transform the project, very subtly so as not to give the game away, in order to make it less threatening towards themselves, as Israel's leaders, and less weak-kneed towards the Gentile enemy. Portraying themselves authoritatively as 'the ordained priests of the elect', they defined Israel's task as the actual construction of 'The Kingdom of God' itself. This was to be achieved by getting the community to live together, *obediently*, according to the blue-print revealed to the prophets, and especially the prophet Ezekiel, who seems to have been the first great leader of the revisionist movement.

Perhaps you are having a little difficulty in distinguishing between these two endeavours? If so, it is a tribute to the biblical editors' work for they did not want readers of the Bible to perceive the difference ... even though, ideologically speaking, it is quite massive. So, let us dwell on it just a few moments longer.

The revolutionary Hebrew endeavour is characteristically *non-authoritarian* since it depends entirely on these marginals' freely given commitment symbolised in the covenant partnership[23]. It is also *non-coercive* since it operates entirely by shaming. Finally, it also comes *without guarantees* since it always remains Yahweh's business to actually bring in the Kingdom ... by softening Gentile hearts[24].

On the other hand, the conservative revisionists' endeavour is characteristically *authoritarian*, working as it does on principles of leadership and obedience. It is also characteristically *coercive* in that Yahweh is always there in the background ready to interfere and bang heads together (thus justifying those who do the same thing 'in his name'). Finally, it characteristically comes with an absolute guarantee, for the blue-print[25], having been magically revealed, is already there simply waiting to be put into effect[26]. This means that in the present moment God's Kingdom supposedly stands ready to be built since it does not involve Yahweh's softening of Gentile hearts and simply depends on Israel's blind obedience in carrying out instructions.

Do you clearly see the difference now?

3) Jesus the True Hebrew Revolutionary

It is clear that in Jesus' own day the revisionists ruled the roost. They were Matthew's 'Pharisees and Sadducees' (Matthew 3:7) and Luke's 'crowd' (Luke 3:7): people who thought they were safely on the right side purely and simply because they were 'children of Abraham'. However, it's just as clear that Jesus himself was a true, god-of-the-marginals revolutionary since he made it his business to fulfil the revolutionary Hebrew dream (the Law and the Prophets). This explains why he began by calling on his fellowcountrymen to join with him in putting on this demonstration of 'loving God (the god of the marginals) and the neighbour as the self', so that Yahweh could finally do his bit: softening Gentile hearts thereby bringing in the Kingdom itself.

John as a God-of-the-Marginals Revolutionary

OK, that is where Jesus stood but where did John the Baptist put himself in this ideological confrontation? We don't have to look very far to find an answer, for this is what he had to say to the 'crowd' of 'Pharisees and Sadducees' when they came to see what he was up to:

You brood of vipers! Who warned you to flee from the coming wrath? Produce fruit in keeping with repentance. And do not think you can say to yourselves, 'We have Abraham as our father.' I tell you that out of these stones God can raise up children for Abraham. The axe is already at the root of the trees, and every tree that does not produce good fruit will be cut down and thrown into the fire. (Matthew 3:7-10)

I'm sure you'll agree that leaves us in absolutely no doubt that John is here taking a revolutionary line against these revisionist nationalists and claiming that the Kingdom has little to do with who you are and everything to do with how you perform.

John's Problem with Jesus

So far so good. But if, like Jesus, John too was a god-of-the-marginals revolutionary and had no ideological bone to pick with Jesus, what then was his gripe? Well, it seems to me that John's difficulty had to do with Jesus' *strategy*. He seems to be telling Jesus in no uncertain terms that he had better pull his finger out and get on with the job of being a god-of-the-marginals militant. You have to remember that John, locked up in prison as a consequence of his revolutionary activity and with no likelihood of ever getting out, must have been anxiously looking to Jesus to produce results since he himself could no longer make a significant contribution. In his place we, too would surely have been looking for eye-catching national events as proof that Jesus was taking his revolutionary job seriously. However, all John got through the reports of his disciples was silence. Understandably, he must have wondered what on earth Jesus was playing at.

Jesus' Riposte

Interestingly, Jesus sends no reply but simply instructs John's disciples to tell their master what they have witnessed:

Jesus replied, "Go back and report to John what you hear and see: The blind receive sight, the lame walk, those who have leprosy are cured, the deaf hear, the dead are raised, and the good news is preached to the poor. Blessed is the man who does not fall away on account of me." (Matthew 11:6)

What we have here is a list of different categories of healing miracles, culminating in a striking god-of-the-marginals declaration: good news being preached to the poor. In this way, Jesus flags up his conviction that, in his activities, Israel's marginals are effectively now being welcomed back into the community as full members. (We must always remember that the poor in the Gospels are not our poor, i.e. those at the bottom of society, but rather the destitute, which is to say those effectively outside society altogether.)

Did Jesus Consider Himself as a Magician?

It's not difficult to understand why Jesus would have considered that his own welcoming of civilisation-rejects back into the revolutionary god-of-the-marginals community was a sign that Isaiah's demonstration-strategy (Israel performing as the light to lighten the Gentiles) had now been set in train ... at least as far as Jesus' personal influence extended. It is, however, more difficult to understand why he would have thought that an ability to change peoples' personal fortunes by healing them in large numbers on the spot, if that is indeed was what was happening, was especially significant. After all, Israel's' job as the servant of Yahweh had never been about the performance of magic. And there's an added problem with this magic business for had Jesus been in the habit of performing large numbers of healing miracles, John would most certainly have heard about them and would not have needed to ask his question about Jesus being 'the one'. So we have to suppose either that John had indeed heard about certain magical performances ... and thought them irrelevant or, more likely, that the actions which the Gospels present as miracles were not the spectacular redressing of individual bad luck we take them to be but rather something inherently political even if discrete. Please note that I am not saying here that the evangelists got it wrong. What I am suggesting is that in reading the miracle stories as magical events we are the ones badly misunderstanding what the evangelists were trying to tell people.

I am aware some will accuse me of trying to 'get round' the miracles and of reducing them to make Jesus acceptable to our modern scientific mindset. However, this is not the case. I don't believe in magic, that is true, but it is not my point. My point is that whether the evangelists believed in magic or not they clearly weren't intent on presenting Jesus as a miracle-worker in the sense of one who can use the power of God to redress people's medical misfortune. For such an understanding turns everything they say into unbelievable nonsense. It simply doesn't make sense to claim that Jesus' spectacular power to redress people's medical misfortune proved his messianic credentials: for redressing peoples' bad luck does not of itself *change society and put it on a proper footing*, which was what the Messiah was supposed to do.

What Were the Signs of the Coming Kingdom for Isaiah

So what was Jesus doing which made him speak about the blind receiving their sight and the lame walking ... etc? Well, we know that Jesus sought to gather faithful Israelites so that they could together perform as Yahweh's 'light' in accordance with the Isaianic formulation of the Hebrew strategy. So, perhaps we should see what the text has to say as regards the signs which would accompany such a demonstration. This is what First Isaiah said:

Strengthen the feeble hands,
steady the knees that give way;
say to those with fearful hearts,
"Be strong, do not fear;

your God will come,
he will come with vengeance;
with divine retribution
he will come to save you."

Then will the eyes of the blind be opened
and the ears of the deaf unstopped.
Then will the lame leap like a deer,
and the mute tongue shout for joy.
Water will gush forth in the wilderness
and streams in the desert. (Isaiah 35.3-4)

"The poor and needy search for water,
but there is none;
their tongues are parched with thirst.
But I the LORD will answer them;
I, the God of Israel, will not forsake them.

I will make rivers flow on barren heights,
and springs within the valleys.
I will turn the desert into pools of water,
and the parched ground into springs." (Isaiah 41:17-18)

And this is Second Isaiah's contribution:

"I, the LORD, have called you in righteousness;
I will take hold of your hand.
I will keep you and will make you
to be a covenant for the people
and a light for the Gentiles,
to open eyes that are blind,
to free captives from prison
and to release from the dungeon those who sit in darkness.

"I am the LORD; that is my name!
I will not give my glory to another
or my praise to idols.
See, the former things have taken place,
and new things I declare;
before they spring into being
I announce them to you.

"I will lay waste the mountains and hills
and dry up all their vegetation;
I will turn rivers into islands
and dry up the pools.
I will lead the blind by ways they have not known,
along unfamiliar paths I will guide them;
I will turn the darkness into light before them
and make the rough places smooth.
These are the things I will do;
I will not forsake them. (Isaiah 42:6-9; 15-16)

And this is what Third Isaiah had to say:

"Behold, I will create
new heavens and a new earth.
The former things will not be remembered,
nor will they come to mind.

But be glad and rejoice forever
in what I will create,
for I will create Jerusalem to be a delight
and its people a joy.
I will rejoice over Jerusalem
and take delight in my people;
the sound of weeping and of crying
will be heard in it no more.

"Never again will there be in it
an infant who lives but a few days,
or an old man who does not live out his years;
he who dies at a hundred
will be thought a mere youth;
he who fails to reach a hundred
will be considered accursed.
They will build houses and dwell in them;
they will plant vineyards and eat their fruit.
No longer will they build houses and others live in them,
or plant and others eat.
For as the days of a tree,
so will be the days of my people;
my chosen ones will long enjoy
the works of their hands.
They will not toil in vain
or bear children doomed to misfortune;
for they will be a people blessed by the LORD,
they and their descendants with them.
Before they call I will answer;
while they are still speaking I will hear.
The wolf and the lamb will feed together,
and the lion will eat straw like the ox,
but dust will be the serpent's food.
They will neither harm nor destroy
on all my holy mountain,"
says the LORD. (Isaiah 65:17-25)

I make no excuse in asking you to read these texts. It is the only way to see that, with the exception of the curing of the leprous, all the 'deficiency' categories which Jesus speaks about (namely, those afflicted by blindness, lameness, deafness, early death and poverty in the sense of marginalisation) are referred to here, along with the basic predatory 'deficiency' found in nature itself (wolves eating lambs and lions devouring oxen). What is more, it is perfectly clear that in these Isaianic texts, these human deficiencies which Jesus is said to miraculously cure are seen as political phenomena and not as diseases which result either from bad genes or bad luck.

Indeed, what all three Isaiahs are saying is that in the Kingdom when it comes, people will be politically aware. They will be ideologically released (from 'prison' and 'the dungeon') and so aware (able to 'see' and 'hear') of what is truly the score rather than being blinded and deafened by their economic interests. More than that, the weak will not be held back by their inherited deficiencies ('lameness' and 'dumbness') but will find ways of fully participating like everyone else. This will mean that the effects of marginalisation (premature death) will cease and marginalisation itself (poverty and need) will disappear.

Jesus Sees Himself to be Performing as Isaiah's True Israel

So isn't it now becoming clear that Jesus must also have been using these deficiencies (blindness, deafness, dumbness, lameness, leprosy and premature death) 'metaphorically' in the very same way, to speak about ideological conditions?

But, I hear you say, what about the leprosy business? Why has this been added? Well, of course, we know that such skin diseases can be very infectious, causing sufferers to be excluded or marginalised from society. So it would have been natural for Jesus to use leprosy as a way of summarising the ideological power against which he was struggling. Indeed, had Jesus simply been listing his record of miraculous cures for physical and psychosomatic disorders, wouldn't we have expected to find demon possession on the list, rather than leprosy, for he clearly was well known as an exorcist? So this, too, strongly indicates that he was deliberately echoing the words of Isaiah and using this list of deficiencies to refer metaphorically to the various ways in which people found themselves ideologically bound. If this indeed was the case then John the Baptist, on receiving the witnesses of his disciples, would perfectly have understood what Jesus had been doing and, just possibly, he would have been reassured.

John Stands Corrected

But if that deals with John's criticism of Jesus what about Jesus' implied criticism of John?

> Blessed is the man who does not fall away on account of me.

It seems to me that though John was certainly a true revolutionary in rejecting both the revisionists' nationalism and their supposition that they were capable of building the Kingdom of God themselves, he was none the less guilty of a lack of trust in the Hebrew shaming strategy. For although he did not make Ezekiel's mistake of believing that Israel had the authority to impose the Kingdom, he clearly did believe that, through his messiah, Yahweh was about to do just that himself ... which, at the end of the day, comes to pretty much the same thing:

> The axe is already at the root of the trees, and every tree that does not produce good fruit will be cut down and thrown into the fire. (Matthew 3:10)

This appeal to an intervening head-banging god standing ready in the background shows that John was, without justification, anticipating a dramatic and violent change and so was unable to see and appreciate what Jesus was, in fact, doing. Indeed, we know from the Jewish historian, Josephus that John, with his revolutionary fervour and belief in a God who was capable of bringing about change by force, made a far greater impact on people in his day than Jesus did. In fact, it was only as a result of the resurrection ... whatever that was ... that this situation changed. When Jesus spoke to his disciples (after those of John had left) of people finding his work a 'stumbling block', he was getting them to understand that they should firmly stick with the Hebrew's shaming strategy and its hope-against-hope that Yahweh would vindicate by softening Gentile hearts. He was letting them know that they should not be tricked by the understandable doubts everyone shares about the god of the marginals and his shaming strategy. They should not, like John, foolishly search for guarantees by envisaging, in place of the god of the marginals, an authoritarian God who operates by banging heads together.

12

The Feeding of the Five Thousand (Mark 6.30-44, Matthew14:13-21, Luke 9:10-17, John 6:1-15)

Israel Needs Reminding of Her Covenant Commitment

The 'Miracle of Sharing' Reading as a Scandal

When it comes to investigating the Bible I'm a great believer in dialogue. So I have decided to use a Catholic blog I recently came across on the web as a sort of dialogue partner in this study[27]. The blog in question belongs to Jimmy Akin who comes from Texas and is the Director of Apologetics and Evangelisation in an organisation called 'Catholic Answers'. This is how he set the ball rolling:

Right now in the Sunday liturgy we're working our way through John 6 ... Last Sunday contained the feeding of the 5,000, and I was annoyed when the priest at the Mass I was attending emphasized a perceived "sharing" aspect of the passage. He didn't go so far as to fully subvert the miracle. That is, he didn't say that it was a "miracle of sharing" where people's hearts were moved to share what they had rather than hoarding it for themselves—a repudiation of the physical miracle that occurred. But he seemed to be skirting the edge of that idea, without saying anything that would explicitly mandate this interpretation. What he did do was emphasize the idea of sharing, and particularly the generosity of the little boy with the five loaves and two fishes. What I find annoying is all the confident talk about how the miracle occurred because the little boy was selflessly willing to share his lunch. Not only does that make it sound like God's omnipotence would have been hamstrung if the little boy had said no, and thus giving the little boy's action way too much credit in an ontological sense, it's also giving the little boy undeserved credit in the generosity department.

A Quick Sale not Generosity

Jimmy goes on to question whether there is any justification in talking about the little boy's generosity, arguing that, given the quantity of food, five pittas and two fishes, it was far too much to constitute a lunch generously shared with others. Jimmy claims the text reads much better if we take it that the boy had been using the occasion to sell his wares and the disciples had bought the food from him for their own consumption. He continues in this vein:

> Of course, the above doesn't amount to a *proof*. It *could* be that the little boy had brought a surprisingly large amount of food for himself and then, for unknown reasons, mentioned this to Andrew and then generously shared it with Jesus and the disciples. *But this isn't the way the text reads.* And it's just annoying when preachers get so wrapped up in a sickly sweet, Hallmark-card spirituality that they go off rhapsodising about human sharing and generosity in a way that flies in the face of the text. The point here is that *God did a miracle through Jesus*, not that a little boy was generous.

The blog then continues with a fair number of people writing in to recount similar experiences of preachers using this sharing angle to 'explain' the miracle and their negative reactions to such sermons:

> Oh man, I so agree with you, Jimmy! We get the same exact homily — all the way over here in India, year after year! They must be reading it online somewhere as they "prepare" for their homily. It totally undermines The Miracle. (Georgette)

AMEN!!! I also received (again) the same cold pablum (baby-food) sermon on Sunday. Thank you for your explanation on this AWESOME miracle of our Lord. (Theresa)

We have a new deacon and his first homily was last week. We got the full blown "shared, previously hidden, group lunch" deal. No apologies from this guy. I came to this parish 14 years ago to escape such Amchurch lunacy and here comes John Shelby Spong in disguise! (Pete)

Yes, I heard the same homily about how it was a miracle that people didn't keep the food to themselves. It seemed as if the priest was downplaying the whole event. I really think that the Lord performed a miracle of multiplication. (Ty)

I was blessed ... not only did our priests stress the miraculous nature of the events, they actually said that the renderings by 'some misguided scholars' to make it into a 'miracle of sharing' was BALDERDASH. (Kate)

What Name for this Despicable New Tendency?

Not unnaturally, the bloggers have different names for this new tendency that has suddenly appeared in their midst and which they don't like in the least. Jimmy Akin himself labels it 'a sickly sweet, Hallmark card spirituality'. Pete above calls it 'Amchurch lunacy' which he associates with the retired Episcopalian bishop John Shelby Spong. Another blogger by the name of EaglesNest speaks of 'the hoky, always feel good, commercial homilies that are all fluff'. All of this is very evocative but it doesn't go far in identifying the political ideology responsible for their woes. Two other bloggers have a stab at being more precise. One, calling himself 'the masked chicken' speaks of it as 'materialist' while the other, who has the initials SDG, labels it 'modernist'.

That said there are two bloggers who do take the analysis a

little bit further. One identifies a well known Scottish Presbyterian Biblicist, the late William Barclay, as the likely source of this mischief, quoting him in full:

> There are those who see in this miracle something which in a sense is perfectly natural, and yet which in another sense is a real miracle, and which in any sense is very precious. Picture the scene. There is a crowd; it is late, and they are hungry. But was it really likely that the vast majority of that crowd would set out around the lake without any food at all? Would they not take something with them, however little? Now it was evening and they were hungry. But they were also selfish. And no one would produce what they had, in case they had to share it and left themselves without enough. Then Jesus took the lead. Such as he and his disciples had, he began to share with a blessing and an invitation and a smile. And thereupon all began to share, and before they knew what was happening, there was enough and more than enough for all.
>
> If this is what happened, it was not the miracle of the multiplication of loaves and fishes; it was the miracle of the changing of selfish people into generous people at the touch of Christ. It was the miracle of the birth of love in grudging hearts. It was the miracle of changed men and women with something of Christ in them to banish their selfishness. If that is so, then in the realest sense Christ fed them with himself and sent his Spirit to dwell within their hearts.
>
> It does not matter how we understand this miracle. One thing is sure - when Christ is there, the weary find rest and the hungry soul is fed" (William Barclay, *The Gospel of Matthew: Chapters 11-28*, pp. 120-121)

The other blogger, by the name of Rosemarie, for her part, tries to analyse the motives driving this ideology:

I think it's more than just the desire to downplay the miraculous and supernatural - though that's no doubt part of it. ... It has more to do with the Eucharistic implications of the miracle. Some Modernists want to replace belief in transubstantiation and the Holy Sacrifice of the Mass with a mere 'celebration of community.' They downgrade the multiplication of the loaves and fish from a supernatural miracle to a natural 'communal sharing' event because it fits that agenda. If the **true** miracle of the loaves and fishes was a 'miracle of sharing' rather than a supernatural multiplication of bread, then the **true** miracle of the Mass is also a 'miracle of sharing' in a gathered community, rather than transubstantiation.

Liberalism as the New Tendency

This is all very suggestive but what exactly is going on? It seems to me that what we are faced with in this blog is quite straightforward. It's simply a very understandable conservative reaction against a new liberal tendency which has begun to appear within the American Catholic Church, the bloggers themselves constituting the conservative reaction and the preachers they object to constituting this new liberal tendency.

The Bloggers as Conservative Catholics...

The Bloggers as Conservative Catholics ... But how can I justify such labels ... and how does giving such labels help us? Well, conservative ideology operates by establishing a structure of authority which people adhere to willingly and obey. You can see this clearly manifest amongst the bloggers who have all consented to a structure of authority, the Catholic Church, and who now expect its officers (priests and deacons) to provide a faithful exposition of the authorised conservative understanding of scripture, an understanding which justifies the Papal Magisterium, Transubstantiation, the Holy Sacrifice of the Mass and, of course, miracles as *true* miracles.

Worried by Liberal Protestantism

Liberal ideology, on the other hand, operates to promote free competition. Its concern is to challenge and remove all arbitrary restrictions, whether imposed from above by conservative establishments or from beneath by revolutionary socialists. In the case of this blog, the offending restriction which the new liberal clerics are questioning is the above conservative understanding that biblical miracles have to be seen as out-of-this-world magic or, as the 'masked chicken' himself so succinctly put it:

> re-arranging matter to make bread and fish that did not already exist.

But what is it that might offend liberals about this magical understanding of scripture ... and how could it be experienced as restrictive?

The answer has to do with the question of relevance. Relevance is the watchword of all liberal exegesis of scripture. For, as liberals see it, if what scripture says is not relevant to people then, in so far as people are subjected to it, scripture inevitably becomes something arbitrarily imposed on them. From a liberal point of view it does not greatly matter whether such imposed restrictions are resisted by people or, as is the case with these Catholic bloggers, gladly accepted by them. For liberals, restrictions of any sort have to be subverted and removed because what matters above everything else is the freedom to compete in life without restrictions. Where the Bible is concerned this can only be done by making the miracles relevant, which means explaining away their magical characteristics ... gently at first because Catholicism, even in the twenty-first century, is still a bastion of conservative ideology.

Truth Defined as Faithfulness to Scripture

Needless to say, our conservative bloggers don't conduct their case against their liberal opponents by the use of straightforward political terminology. Indeed, they confine their arguments strictly to the question of which side is being most faithful to scripture.

The Miracle of Sharing Rightly Denounced
as Unscriptural

The bloggers do an impressive job in demolishing the miracle-of-generosity-and-sharing interpretation by showing how it traduces the texts. It's not just that the texts do not naturally read as miracles of generosity and sharing. It's also that the generosity and sharing understanding doesn't fit either with the way Jesus speaks about the need to purchase food or, indeed, with the reports of the large amount of leftovers:

> ... what did they do with the leftovers? If there had been 'sharing,' wouldn't people have asked for doggie bags? (The Masked Chicken)

In fact, it is quite plain that no miracle of generosity and sharing is to be found in the actual text, which means that to find it you have to read it in-between the lines. This is simply not admissible because, of course, you can turn a text completely against itself if you are allowed to read things between the lines. For example, commentators nowadays, *reading between the lines,* are inclined to say that this text betrays the early Church's interest in the Eucharist. This would seem to me to be nonsense for how could what is actually *written on the lines* (that there were five loaves and two fishes) possibly mean anything in a Eucharistic setting where the singular body of Christ is represented by a single loaf of bread?

But is the Miracle as Heavenly Magic any
More Scriptural?

However, though our bloggers experience no difficulty in

demonstrating the glaring inadequacies in the way in which their ideological opponents interpret this story, they seem strangely blind to the glaring inadequacies in their own magical interpretations. Let me use one of the blogs to demonstrate this point:

It always seemed to me that this particular miracle was one of the harder ones to visualize. How, exactly, did it look? Were they working their way through the crowd tearing off chunks of the loaves and what was left in their hands just regenerated before their eyes? Were they handing them out from a sack of some sort and every time they reached in there was more than before? At Cana there were jugs of water and the next time they checked them they had wine. No less spectacular or significant but it's easy to visualize the narrative. Jesus touches someone and they heal, etc. I can picture how those would look if you were present at the time. But here, the act of multiplication, right before the eyes of everyone in attendance, seems so extraordinary and yet so linguistically banal, with a narrative style that seems almost deliberately vague. 'He took five loaves and two fish and fed 5000'. Wait. What? I wonder if that narrative style is the stumbling block for some people that gives rise to the 'sharing' interpretation. (Bill)

I find this comment, coming as it does from someone who basically goes along with the miracle-as-magic proposition, curiously honest yet disconcerting. What surprises is that having conclusively put his own magical understanding of the story out of court (for how can you possibly be expected to believe in a event that you can't even begin to imagine) he then tries to come to terms with the impact of what he has just divulged by reducing it to a problem of style, suggesting that had the style of narration been different, the miracle itself would have been somehow more believable. In terms of what he has said, this is all too absurd for if you can't even manage to imagine a bit of magic then describing it differently is surely not going to make any difference.

Jesus' Miracles as Lacking in Persuasiveness

Interestingly, the Gospels relate that not even the disciples were convinced by Jesus' miracles and it was only with the resurrection that things changed. This makes it difficult to argue that Jesus' miracles were designed to make people believe. Because of this, I find the following contribution very interesting:

> I have always felt that the miraculous nature of the event is vindicated by its failure: presented with this amazing performance, the people completely miss the point and try to make Jesus a king, for which reason he flees from them. Politicians make their careers by providing the goods like this, but Jesus wanted no part of that kind of power. The meaning of the event is provided by his Eucharistic teaching: "I Am the Bread of Life" —a teaching even his closest disciples would not begin to grasp until he broke bread on the night before he died. Miracles are not merely raw exercises of power, they have always a teaching function. The contribution of the boy may simply be that A: grace works through nature (and all that implies) and B: miracles validate faith. Jesus' miracles always occur in the presence of faith, validating those who put their trust —however tentatively — in Him. Notably, Jesus could work few miracles among his own village and people. (Mike Walsh)

I agree that some of Jesus' miracles seem to validate faith but what does 'validating faith' mean in the case of this story? Is Mike really suggesting Jesus performed this miracle to justify the little boy's faith in him? There is no evidence the little boy expressed any faith, as Jimmy Akin himself is the first to point out. And even if we grant the little boy in John's story did have faith, whose faith was validated in the other accounts where the little boy makes no appearance? It seems to me that here again we find these conservative bloggers trying to deal with a crucial problem that appears to blow their whole approach clean out of the water, by simply declaring that a thing must be true since it gives every appearance of being untrue. Again if, like these conservative bloggers, you adopt a miracle-as-magic approach to these texts you then have a serious problem explaining why, after Jesus had miraculously fed five thousand men in one remote spot, his disciples didn't realise what was coming a few days later when the same problem arose with four thousand men, in another remote spot:

> During those days another large crowd gathered. Since they had nothing to eat, Jesus called his disciples to him and said, 'I have compassion for these people; they have already been with me three days and have nothing to eat. If I send them home hungry, they will collapse on the way, because some of them have come a long distance.' His disciples answered, "But where in this remote place can anyone get enough bread to feed them?" (Mark 8:1-4)

You can't have it both ways. If all of these miracles were indeed the mind-blowing magical feats these bloggers take them to have been, then everyone, and most certainly Jesus' disciples, would have believed, for belief in such circumstances would have been easy and would have come quite naturally. Consequently, the fact that all the evangelists maintain that even the disciples themselves did not believe can only indicate *that the evangelists were not talking about out-of-this-world magic*.

Liberal and Conservative Readings Both Equally Flawed

It would seem therefore that the traditional conservative under-standing of this text is just as flawed as the liberal interpretation which seeks to replace it. This being the case, how are we now to understand the story in a way that is both fundamentally faithful to the text, yet at the same time sees the story itself as perfectly relevant to our modern mindset and situation?

The Marginal Reading: The Miracle as Symbolic

Let me put before you what I see as the marginal reading of the story: doesn't the story recount that Jesus fed five thousand people with enough food and to spare, even though they had brought no food for themselves? For five loaves and two fishes is 'no food' for five thousand people, wouldn't you say? Given that Mark 8:14-21 makes it clear this story is symbolic, doesn't this make you think that 'food' here must mean 'ideological food'? If this is the case then isn't the story ever so clearly saying Jesus found, unsurprisingly, that these Israelites who, if you will remember, he was asking to join him in performing as Yahweh's light, had no understanding of their god-of-the-marginals covenant commitment. They were, therefore, just like us ... ideologically bankrupt ... only, unlike us, they were unhappy with their state. For, whether we are conservative, liberal or socialists, as comfortable Christians, we think we know it all. So if we had happened to have been around at that time we would most probably have stayed comfortably at home, not bothering to journey with Jesus into the wilderness to rediscover the truth! But, as I have explained, these five thousand were the riff-raff and they knew they needed ideological food. And Jesus fed them, explaining to them their god-of-the-marginals tradition, which is to say the Law and the Prophets: the five loaves symbolising the Pentateuch and the two fishes symbolising Moses and Elijah. And at the end when they were fed, there were twelve baskets of food left over ... which is to say *enough to go on and feed the whole of Israel*: the twelve symbolising the twelve tribes.

But Nobody Wants to Know

It would appear, therefore, that the story is simply a way of recounting Jesus' campaign and it does so wonderfully well, don't you think? But do most of us see it? No, we don't! Instead we spend our time transforming it so as to deal with the story's magic which, though it is merely symbolic, either worries or enchants us. And the fact that any new version of the story, whether conservative or liberal, does not fit with the text is of no consequence *since it now says what we want to hear rather than the awful truth about our bankrupt selves which the god of the marginals exposes.*

13

The Syro-Phoenician Woman (Mark 7:27-28, Matthew 15:26-27)

The Revolutionary Strategy Collides with the Faith of a Gentile.

Not Just Another Healing

This story involves a miraculous healing: an exorcism to be precise. That said, its purpose can hardly have been to highlight Jesus' ability to transform human situations, as so many people have wrongly supposed, since in the story this is simply taken for granted. It seems to me, therefore, that the story can only have been designed to draw attention to two things:

1. Jesus' strategy, which involved prioritising contacts with fellow Jews.
2. The gentile woman's astonishing straightforwardness and lack of hypocrisy: the characteristic which Jesus described as faith.

Restricting ourselves to the elements that are common to both Mark and Matthew, we are presented with this little gem:

Jesus left that place and withdrew to the vicinity of Tyre. A foreign woman from that region came to him begging him to drive out a demon that had taken possession of her daughter.

'It is not right to take the children's bread and toss it to the dogs' he told her.

'Yes, Lord, but even the dogs under the table eat the children's crumbs' she replied.

'For such a reply, you may go; the demon has left your daughter.' he said and from that hour she was healed.

A Badly Treated Foreign Woman?

Since this text deals with the fate of a foreign woman it's hard not to compare it with the story of Ruth, (which unfortunately there has not been space to study in this book). Such a comparison raises two major problems. First, given the book of Ruth's trenchant defense of foreigners, and foreign *women* in particular, how can one explain why Jesus in this story appears to begin by raising an objection and refusing to help the Syro-Phoenician woman? Second, why does Jesus apparently go out of his way to liken the woman to a dog, a spurious insult one might surely justifiably claim? You can't help suspecting that if Luke made no use of this text in his Gospel it was because he found the incident inherently distasteful.

The Atheist Reading

People tend to deal with these problems differently, depending on their outlooks. *Atheists*, for example, will seize on them in order to try and make out that Jesus was no paragon of political virtue, being just as bigoted and uncaring where foreigners were concerned as everyone else in his day. But such an argument shows no real attempt to understand what the text, with its important strategic language, is trying to put across. This is an error shared by *fundamentalist Christians*, the atheists' implacable foe, who simply deny that the text contains any strategic language needing to be understood. But superficially at least, as we shall see, atheists do seem to have a point ... of sorts.

The Conservative Reading

Others come up with different ways of understanding Jesus' words depending on their ideological perspectives. Given the conservative Israelite view already found in the Bible's revisionist texts (namely that Israel was a holy nation chosen by Yahweh to be his people) it's natural to find *conservative Christians* arguing that this was Jesus' own point of view. It's understandable therefore if they go on to try and find ways of justifying Jesus' apparently questionable behaviour. They point out, for example, that the political relationship between Israel and these Lebanese foreigners had always been strained (as indeed still is the case today) and then go on to recount in gory detail all the atrocities which the inhabitants of Tyre and Sidon had committed against the Jews in the immediate past. The argument is that though Israel was certainly not a perfect community, she was spiritually (and so politically) far superior to her Gentile neighbours. This explains why Jesus took the trouble to draw this Gentile woman's attention to her spiritual uncleanness (i.e. second class standing) by likening her position to that of a dog. Such a view not only makes out that Jesus' conduct was perfectly justified but goes further, implying it was, in fact, the right and proper thing to do. When it comes to Jesus' apparent change of mind in the face of the woman's determined persistence, this is not identified as weakness but rather as an act of gracious, conservative conde-scension in which Jesus rewards the woman for her open acknowledgement of her unclean, doglike, second-class state, by finally giving her what she craves.

The Liberal Reading

Liberal Christians, for their part, sensibly do not try to defend the politically indefensible in this woeful manner. Instead they are more likely to suggest that Jesus never refused to help the woman but was simply testing her. At the same time they tend to do all they can to soften the 'dog' insult by pointing out that the actual word Jesus used was not 'dog' but rather the diminutive 'puppy'. Further to this, instead of concentrating on the static 'cleanness and uncleanness' aspect of the story, as conservatives do, liberals are happier to interpret it dynamically in terms of frontier-crossing: Jesus crosses into the woman's Syro-Phoenician territory and then the woman herself returns the complement by, metaphorically, crossing into Jesus' Israelite territory. In this way liberals are able to interpret the story as having to do with the surmounting of an arbitrary, man-made barrier which was restricting people from spreading their wings and enjoying themselves in life's naturally free and competitive environment. But the trouble with such an explanation, as many have pointed out, is that calling a woman 'a little bitch' is scarcely any better than calling her 'a bitch'. Furthermore, isn't it stretching things somewhat to pretend that Jesus and the woman were motivated by the spirit of free enterprise which drives modern society? *Naturally, liberal commentators don't talk about the market economy when analysing this story. Rather they write in vague ethical terms about a liberal spirit which comes from Jesus and which frees people to be their true selves:*

> ... Jesus ... encourages me to celebrate life, to suck the marrow out of existence, to explore, and probe, and experiment, to venture into uncharted seas, without fear of a tyrannical and vindictive God. He does not set limits on my curiosity, on my drive to challenge every axiom. That same Jesus prompts me to give myself to tasks that exceed, even contradict, my own self-interest. I am not infrequently startled at the tasks I find myself willing to undertake. (R.W. Funk; *Honest to Jesus* Harper Collins 1996, p.19)

In this way they camouflage where they are coming from for they know only too well that people are never going to believe that crude economic liberalism can be found in the Bible.

The Radical (Socialist) Reading

When it comes to *radical Christians*, like feminists for instance, they often take this revolutionary liberal argument even further. They agree that the 'dog' saying was indeed insulting and inadmissible, claiming that, at the beginning of his encounter with the Syro-Phoenician woman, Jesus was un-self-critically ethnocentric. Their approach is that the woman's altogether unexpected and, indeed, mind boggling reply forced Jesus to undergo a change of heart. And it is this which was largely responsible for his dawning recognition that the Gentiles, although they were indeed outsiders, also had their rightful place in the Kingdom. On this reading, the supposedly conservative Jesus does not know what to do when he is confronted with a Gentile woman asking for his help, but his hesitancy is eventually blown away by the sheer *chutzpah* of her retort. This being the case, Jesus' greatness is not seen to lie in always being right (a proposition we moderns, with our ideas about progress and development, find difficult to accept) but, rather, in being continuously open to revolutionary change. I have to admit I like this reading of the story and really wish it was viable. However, sadly it isn't: though scholars have often tried to make out Jesus was forced to change his strategy, the truth is there is not a scrap of evidence for this in the Gospels. These portray him, rightly or wrongly, as never deviating one instant from his chosen path since he was perfectly aware from the very beginning where he was going and was always in total command of the situation. Undoubtedly, it can be argued that the evangelists masked a change of strategy which we can now only 'witness' by reading in between the lines of their texts. However, such an argument is very tiresome because anything can be proved by reading between the lines. *On* the lines, there is simply no room for a change of strategy. Consequently I find myself rejecting this radical interpretation even more vehemently than I did the previous liberal one, precisely because I like the picture it paints.

The Proper Marginal Reading

As I see it, the trouble with all of the above interpretations is that they fail to take on board the big picture of what Jesus' was attempting to do and instead try to make the story fit (or in the case of Atheists, misfit) with some accepted modern political perspective. So let us see now what happens if we view this story from the Bible's own marginal perspective in which, according to Isaiah, the task of all true Israelites was to shame the world into changing its ways by collectively putting on a demonstration of what it meant to live together in radical solidarity, banishing marginality from their midst by loving the neighbour as the self. As soon as we do this it immediately becomes clear what Jesus was up to: he was calling on *his fellow Israelites* to join him in putting on this Isaianic demonstration, declaring that the time had come to do the necessary so that God could finally bring in his kingdom. This explains why, when the cured demon-possessed foreigner in Mark 5 asked Jesus if he could follow him, Jesus refused and told him to go back to his family. It also explains why Jesus made no attempt to take his message to mixed Jewish-Gentile communities in Palestine (such as the major town of Sepphoris which, though just round the corner from Nazareth, never gets a mention in the Gospels) but rather targeted areas where Jews were living together. It even explains why Matthew, in his version of this story, has Jesus add the rider that he was sent *only* to the lost sheep of the house of Israel. And it also, finally, explains why Mark has Jesus insist, 'First let the children eat all they want'. The point here is that after Jesus had fulfilled the Isaianic strategy, having to act on his own because everyone else had deserted him, things inevitably changed: *for the crucial demonstration had now taken place leaving no strategic reason for Gentiles to be treated differently.*

Jesus helps the Woman see His Difficulties and She Helps Him see Hers

So you see when you adopt this marginal perspective everything in the story is seen to hang together very nicely. But what effect does it have on those two problems we spoke about earlier?

1. Why did Jesus begin by raising an objection and refusing to

help the woman?

2. Why did he insult her by likening her position to that of a dog?

Well, if we take it that Jesus' crossing of the frontier with his disciples was a tactical move designed to momentarily take the pressure off their situation, as Mark seems to imply:

> Jesus left that place and went to the vicinity of Tyre. He entered a house and did not want anyone to know it; yet he could not keep his presence secret. (Mark. 7:24)

It becomes obvious why the foreign woman's request presented him with a problem. For to grant it would clearly involve Jesus in going outside his strategic remit of putting on a demonstration *together with other Israelites*. Of course, he could not expect such a woman to appreciate this strategy, or its importance to him for that matter, so to answer her at all inevitably meant using all of his ingenuity to try and get her to see just as much of his predicament as was possible. He attempted to do this, as was his wont, by means of a parable, for parables are expressly designed *to open peoples' eyes and get them to see things they are not seeing*. In this parable a family's overriding strategic duty to use its scarce food resources exclusively to feed its children is used to bring into focus his own overriding strategic duty to use his own resources exclusively in getting his fellow Israelites to join with him in creating a shaming demonstration: a process which logically excluded foreigners like the Syro-Phoenician woman. Clearly the woman instantly saw the point he was making, without necessarily understanding all of the intricacies of the marginal strategy itself. She did not take offence, as we probably would have done, supposing Jesus was insulting her. If we make such mistakes it is only because we know nothing of parables and so confuse likenesses with symbols. This leads us to see Jesus as *symbolically calling the woman a dog* when in fact all he was doing was *likening her position to that of a family dog whose needs manifestly have less priority than those of the children.* The beauty of the parable is that anyone can see that children have to be given priority over dogs. Because of this, the Syro-Phoenician woman was able in a flash to give Jesus her reposte, in which she turns the parable around and uses it to illuminate her own situation *for him.* As she sees things, she is faced with the absolute necessity of scandalously defying every civilised convention in order to seize this once-in-a-lifetime opportunity created by Jesus' tactical withdrawal to her locality. So she turns his parable, which was about 'overriding strategic priorities', into a new parable, which is now about 'absolutely un-missable opportunities', in order to open *his* eyes to the fact that she has been *obliged* by the desperation of her plight (whatever this was) to throw all civilised conventions to the wind and find *any means she can* of addressing him *personally* ... as *a man* ... and worse still ... as *a foreigner* ... even if it means ... horror of horrors ... infringing *the privacy of his abode.*

Faith, a Political Virtue, Lauded

The result of this speech is quite inevitable, for here, according to Matthew, is faith which Jesus on another occasion (see Matthew 8.10) said he had failed to find amongst his own people: a fact which rather puts a stopper on the risible conservative argument that Jesus saw Israelites, though not perfect, as somehow superior to foreigners! It should be noted that in using the word faith Matthew is not talking about a religious conviction of the sort that; 'if you believe and make Jesus your Lord then you will be saved'. For clearly faith in this story is a secular and political virtue which consists of a studied determination to be straight-forward and open, neither bowing to crippling civilisational conventions on the one hand, nor resorting to bribes or attempting to curry favour on the other. This is not, of course, the way in which Christians habitually use the word faith today. They want to make faith *proactive* by turning it into a positive thing which believers have and unbelievers don't. Understandably atheists find this extraordinarily condescending and rightly so. This sort of proactive faith couldn't be more unlike what Jesus was admiring in the Syro-Phoenician woman. Faith for Jesus was altogether *reactive,* an utter openness to reality and refusal to pretend, as all of us hypocrites do, and there is no hint of condescension or currying favour in that. Given the woman is perfectly straight with Jesus, refusing to play silly games and simply telling him why she has acted in the bold way she has, how can he now refuse? Is it surprising he makes of her an exception ... *the exception*, indeed, *that proves the rule?*

Everything Makes Sense

So you see how it is: when we adopt the marginal perspective and see Jesus as operating with the marginals' shaming strategy, the problems that we have created for ourselves over the years, by trying to read the Gospel texts from our wrong conservative, liberal or socialist perspectives, fall away and we find ourselves *seeing,* and the Gospels *making sense,* even if it is often a revelation of something *we would rather not see* and a sense moreover which *we could well* do *without!*

14

The Transfiguration
(Mark 9:2-13, Matthew 17:1-13,
Luke 9:28-36, 2 Peter 1:17-18)

Jesus as the culmination of the Hebrew/marginal tradition

The Story in Outline

Jesus takes a select group of disciples with him up a mountain where they see him transfigured. Luke says the disciples were a bit dazed as if half asleep and all three evangelists write that Jesus' clothes appeared intensely white while Luke remarks that his face too appeared altered. Further to this, the evangelists recount that it seemed to the disciples that Jesus was in conversation with two men who turned out to be Moses and Elijah, though how the disciples found this out is not explained. As a climax to the event the evangelists describe God speaking out of a low-lying cloud, saying; 'This is my beloved son (Matthew adding 'with whom I am well pleased' and Luke 'my chosen' or 'beloved'); 'listen to him'. An embarrassed Peter is said to have suggested that the disciples should build three booths; one for Jesus and the other two for his guests. All three evangelists relate that the disciples did not speak publicly about this incident while Jesus was alive, Mark and Matthew saying that this was because Jesus had specifically instructed them not to do so until after the resurrection, a statement which naturally puzzled them since clearly the term as yet meant nothing to them. Luke for his part has nothing to say directly about the resurrection though he is the one to indicate that the conversation with Moses and Elijah was about 'a departure which Jesus was to accomplish in Jerusalem' and you may think that this amounts to much the same thing. In Mark and Matthew there is then a conversation on the way back down from the mountain, between Jesus and the disciples, about the belief that Elijah would return. Jesus tells them that this has already taken place, the returned prophet having been put to death, which makes them all think he is referring to John the Baptist.

An Historical Account or a Symbolic Story?

The question is, did the evangelists want their readers to understand this story as an account of an actual incident in Jesus' life or did they expect them to see it as something rather more symbolic: as a way of getting readers to focus on what the evangelists believed was the significance of this extraordinary life? There are three reasons which make me think they meant people to see the story as symbolic. The first is the fact that the evangelist, John, never mentions it. 'So what?' you may say. For why should all the evangelists cover the same ground? This is true, of course, and if we were dealing with just another run of the mill story from the life of Jesus I would not be carping. However, what it relates is altogether extraordinary. For in the Bible it is very rare for Yahweh to make himself directly present, either visibly or audibly, to human beings. I am not referring here to situations where God is said to answer prayer or call on people to perform some service. These sorts of situation are relatively common. What I am talking about are 'face-to-face' encounters with Yahweh which, as such, *confirm people as being true god-of-the-marginals revolutionaries.* As far as I know, there are only six such incidents within the Bible, four in the Old Testament and two in the New. The only other occasion within the Gospels where God is said to speak 'face-to-face' with someone, vindicating them in so doing, is at Jesus' baptism ... a story which this transfiguration piece clearly echoes.

If the Transfiguration Was Historical Why Did John Leave it out?

But don't get me wrong. I'm not suggesting that because God's speech at Jesus' baptism appears in all four gospels it must have been an actual historical event. All I am saying is that had it been known that God had actually appeared and physically vindicated Jesus in front of witnesses, as explained in the transfiguration story, then it is inconceivable that John, or any other evangelists for that matter, would have ignored it when writing his Gospel. In a very similar vein, in relation to the story of Lazarus, which I look at in the next study, I argue that restoring a man to life after he had been rotting in his tomb for three whole days would have constituted such an important occurrence (the medical event of all time indeed) that no self-respecting evangelist would have left it out of his account had he known about it. Consequently, the fact that only John includes it must mean he himself created/introduced it to make some point[28]. So just as I find it impossible to believe that Matthew, Mark and Luke knew about Jesus' raising of Lazarus from the dead but failed to include it in their accounts so too I find it impossible to believe John knew of, yet chose to remain silent about, an occasion when Yahweh spoke audibly, in person and before witnesses, to vindicate Jesus. This consideration on its own would have been enough to convince me that the transfiguration story was meant to be taken as symbolic, but there are other factors which also reinforce this belief.

Viewing the Transfiguration as Historical Just Creates Problems.

A second reason for thinking the story is symbolic is the fact that treating it as an historical event creates more problems than it solves. To begin with, as I have already remarked, no explanation is given as to how the disciples came to realise it was Moses and Elijah they saw talking with Jesus. Next, Mark and Matthew openly admit there is a difficulty about Jesus speaking to the disciples about the resurrection, for naturally enough the disciples could not possibly understand what Jesus was talking about since he had not even died! Furthermore, to make out that Jesus knew he was going to die and be raised leads us into obvious difficulties about special foreknowledge and magical powers, compounded by the fact that the whole scenario is completely at odds with what subsequently happened: Jesus making it quite plain in the garden of Gethsemane that he wished to avoid what seemed to be his approaching fate if it would be at all possible. This is not the thinking of a man who knew he had to die in order to be raised. Worse than that, the idea that Jesus somehow knew he would be raised grossly trivialises the cross by reducing Jesus to a religious martyr whose death was palliated by the fact that he knew he would receive his reward. As the Taliban show us every day, religious martyrs go to their deaths willingly and even to some extent gladly. This does not mean they enjoy dying. It is because they face death certain of a future recompense. It cannot be said enough that Jesus' death was not of this kind ... though it is what this text, if it is taken as an historical event, seems to imply. The full horror of the cross can only be taken on board when you realise that, far from being certain of vindication, Jesus endured it without any guarantee, fully aware that it might all have been in vain: My God! My God! Why have you forsaken me? (Matthew 27:46). Just for the sake of completeness, I should also mention that the very same arguments can be employed in the case of Luke's contention that the subject of the discussion with Moses and Elijah was about 'the departure' that Jesus was about to accomplish in Jerusalem.

It goes without saying that the story of the transfiguration is, intrinsically, not just about Jesus' 'face to face' meeting with Yahweh but also about his connection with Moses and Elijah on the one hand and the resurrection on the other. Yet if we take the story as an account of an actual historical event then Moses, Elijah and the resurrection all appear strangely out of place in it as flies do when they appear in your soup. Of course we could all dream up rational scenarios explaining away these difficulties if we had to, but that is not the point since none of the evangelists bothered their heads about them. Surely this can only mean that they were not writing history on this occasion but rather trying to say something crucially important about this human life.

A Story Made up of Echoes.

A third reason for thinking the story is symbolic is that, apart from Peter's embarrassed remark about making shelters to accommodate Jesus and his two friends, which in itself is intriguing and needs an explanation, the story is made up of nothing but echoes from the four other great, vindicating 'face-to-face' encounters with Yahweh which are found in the Old Testament:

1. The story of Jacob wrestling with the angel (Genesis 32:22-32)
2. The story of God speaking to Job out of the whirlwind (Job 38)
3. The stories of God speaking to Moses in the tabernacle and on Mount Sinai (Exodus 33:9-11, 34:29-31)
4. The story of God speaking to Elijah on Mount Horeb (1 Kings 19:9-13)

Indeed you could say the story of the transfiguration appears to have been concocted with the sole purpose of binding what Jesus (and John the Baptist) had achieved … or was going to achieve in Jerusalem in a few days' time … within this traditional god-of-the-marginals framework. Consequently if we use these stories as spectacles we should be able simply to read off the meaning of the transfiguration itself without any bother. However, to be able to do this we will have to remind ourselves about these four traditional stories. So let's take a quick look without going into too much detail.

The Jacob and Job Stories as Paradigms

The first two stories are very different from the second two in that they deal with representational rather than historical characters. In Story 1, Jacob is clearly a representation of Israel and, as our previous study has led us to believe, in Story 2, Job looks very much like a representation of the post-exilic revolutionary prophetic group. In other words, Stories 1 and 2 constitute paradigms (stories which attempt to map out in general terms the kind of behaviour that god-of-the-Hebrew/marginal revolutionaries should strive to attain) whereas Stories 3 and 4 purport to be accounts of what certain historical individuals actually achieved. So let us look at the paradigms first.

The Jacob Story as the Central Paradigm Setting Out the Hebrew Strategy for World Transformation

The Jacob story (which unfortunately we haven't had a chance to analyse so I would simply ask you to take the results of my research on trust) explains that there is a crucial problem with Israel's performance as Yahweh's servant. Of itself this servanthood guarantees success since it constitutes the proper non-competitive way of living. However, it has one great drawback which is that such success of itself makes other Hebrew communities jealous so that they then try to find ways of doing Israel down. This in turn makes Israel herself react negatively, the net result being a thoroughly unhealthy competitive rivalry which can only be overcome if and when Israel herself manages to achieve humility through hard and painful struggle, thereby getting her performance just right. At the moment when she manages at last to make her behaviour perfectly square with her ideology she becomes, as it were, Yahweh's equal and to her surprise the surrounding communities no longer act jealously towards her but accept her and her success with love and family affection.

The Job Story as a Modification of this Strategy

So the Jacob story sets out the great strategic god-of-the-marginals paradigm lying at the heart of the Bible. However, it does not constitute a last word, for clearly the Job story seeks to modify it in an important respect. As we have seen, the problem the Job story attempts to deal with is the common experience amongst Hebrew/marginal revolutionaries that in spite of their best efforts their enemies' hearts are not softened. In other words, for some reason, Yahweh fails to carry out his promise and withholds success ... a predicament which does not square with the covenant agreement[29]. What the Job story adds to the basic god-of-the-marginals paradigm, therefore, is that if and when Yahweh does not fulfil his side of the covenant bargain, Hebrew revolutionaries must nonetheless persist, believing Yahweh will in time and in person vindicate their efforts, even though it happens beyond the grave by means of something very like resurrection.

The Moses Story: Vindication of What the World Sees as Failure

Taken together we can say that these two stories offer a picture of the Bible's central god-of-the-marginals strategy for transforming the world. What then about the 'historical' stories? Those concerning Moses (two of them: one about Moses talking with Yahweh on a specific occasion on Mount Sinai and the other about Moses' daily talks with Yahweh at the door of the tabernacle) are clearly designed to vindicate his revolutionary marginal behaviour; first by portraying the Hebrew hero as transfigured (his face becoming 'radiant') and then by describing him, not as proving himself Yahweh's equal as in the Jacob story, but rather as becoming Yahweh's personal friend. I find it difficult to think of a more telling way of making the very same point. What's amazing, however, is that while the Moses story as a whole vindicates the hero as 'the top performer' in the role of the god of the marginals' faithful servant, it nonetheless also portrays him as an abysmal failure in the eyes of the civilised world: for at the critical moment it describes him as completely losing his nerve and so forfeiting his right of entry into the promised land. The point being made is that though it may be true that performing as the god-of-the-marginals' faithful servant guarantees a certain success (since that is manifestly how people should behave) this success is not necessarily the same thing as success as the civilised world sees things. Once again what we find here is a slight but significant modification of the Jacob story which, as far as I can see, made no distinction between worldly success and success as seen through the eyes of a marginal.

The Elijah Story: Learning Through Error

Like the account of Moses on Mount Sinai the Elijah story is very obviously concerned with a mountain-top 'face-to-face' encounter with Yahweh. However, when it comes to the crucial business of vindication things are far from clear since it could reasonably be said that this story has more to do with Elijah's correction and instruction than it has to do with his vindication. It makes it clear that unlike Moses, who tended to be hesitant, Elijah's great strength lay in his zeal and daring. The only problem with this was that in the revisionist turmoil into which Ahab's marriage to Jezebel had plunged Israel, Elijah found himself instinctively resorting to *violent* opposition just like any old terrorist. Indeed his bloodthirstiness more than mimicked Moses' own annihilation of his revisionist opponents in Exodus 32.25-29. What the Elijah story does is to get Elijah to see that Yahweh, as god of the marginals, abhors all kinds of violence since his power resides in *reactive* rather than *proactive* force, in the still small voice which shames. Of course vindication does eventually arrive for Elijah, though not in this particular episode, when he is finally taken directly up to heaven in a fiery chariot.

But here that is still a future event rather like the resurrection in the transfiguration story!

Summary

What we find in these four face-to-face-encounter-with-Yahweh stories, which broadly deal with the matter of the Hebrew/marginal strategy for changing the world, is not an immutable blue-print to which all revolutionary behaviour must strictly conform but something infinitely more material and therefore subtle: an ideological strategy in fact. It is this marginal ideology and its strategy which we must now use as spectacles in order to properly read the transfiguration story if we can.

The Meaning of the Transfiguration Story

Yet again we have here a 'face-to-face' encounter with Yahweh taking place on a mountain-top. The only real difference being that unlike the Moses and Elijah stories, the evangelists describe Jesus as taking witnesses with him. In this way they leave readers with the impression that Jesus was somehow already in the know as to what was about to take place. This immediately gives the story an air of unreality, making it quite unlike the Moses and Elijah stories which, if you accept the mythical language in which they are couched, are perfectly realistic.

Now this whole 'face-to-face' mountain-top setting indicates that the evangelists intended that all three stories should be read together. However, they clearly considered that wasn't enough for they proceeded to make the connection with Moses and Elijah unmistakable by actually introducing the two prophets into the story itself. It is interesting to note that in the transfiguration story the god of the marginals, in his 'face-to-face' encounter, vindicates Jesus by calling him his son rather than his faithful servant or friend. This difference is underlined by the absence of any trace of the sort of criticism found in the other two stories. It's not that Jesus achieves a perfect performance without any sort of struggle because he is God incarnate. Far from it! It's just that, unlike what was the case with Moses and Elijah, the performance appears to be without blemish: hence the appellation 'son'. Of course, as in the other stories, the performance is not yet finished. Indeed, the most important part of it is yet to come, which is why vindication, though already pronounced, is also spoken about in terms of resurrection even though this makes the story, once again, difficult to believe as in any way historical. In this connection, see the disciples' expression of bewilderment.

Needless to say, as is almost always the case with this marginal ideology and its thoroughly uncomfortable revelations of human hypocrisy[30], people who wanted to be considered as followers found it impossibly hard to take, making it necessary for them to find some way of toning down its exigencies. Thus it was that Christians later took the classic revisionist way out by turning the whole marginal/ideological construct into religion: deliberately misreading this talk of sonship by taking it literally. In this way they turned the threatening revolutionary marginal ideology into comfortable conservative religion even while pretending to glorify their master thereby! But how can I be so sure the evangelists didn't want people to read their story religiously in the first place? After all it has nothing to say about Jesus' performance, concentrating as it does entirely on his person.

A Religious or Ideological Interpretation

This is an extremely important question and it will be worth thinking about what is entailed before we try to answer it. What is crucial to understand is that we are not dealing here with a straightforward 'either/or' situation for no one is arguing the story is altogether unconcerned with performance. The *ideological* understanding is that because Jesus' performance proved to be perfect he was subsequently declared by his followers to be Yahweh's son, whereas the *religious* understanding is that given that Jesus is God incarnate it stands to reason his performance was perfect. To put it in a nutshell; in the ideological reading performance is primary whereas in the religious reading it is secondary. 'But hold on a minute' you may say (as I have often said to myself!) 'since both understandings see 'performance' and 'person' going together what's the big deal concerning which comes first?' Well, the truth is that the deal could not be more significant or more important: as I have already suggested, a religious reading destroys the exposing marginal, reactive/ shaming approach where performance is the only thing that counts and replaces it with a conservative, proactive/authoritarian approach which is based entirely on personalities ... sons and prophets and so forth. For it reads the texts as if an almighty God is simply sending down to earth his viceroy and commanding people to obey him.

Decision Time

So which is the right reading, conservative religion or revolutionary marginal ideology? Well, fortunately we are not dealing here with just one story. This makes it much easier to decide on the proper understanding. If we read the evangelists' transfiguration story religiously with Jesus 'the son' as a personality associated with the godhead then surely we must also see Moses and Elijah in the same light as personalities associated with the godhead: God's friend and God's servant. But that is absurd for what makes one a friend and the other a servant *if not their performance?* Or are we to suppose that Moses was *born* as God's friend and Elijah as God's servant, just as Jesus was supposedly *born* as the second person of the trinity? That surely can't be right, can it? Frankly I don't think the religious personality approach to the text can stand scrutiny and let us be quite clear what I am saying. I'm not suggesting Christians are wrong in seeing Jesus as God incarnate, for that is a matter entirely up to them. I am saying that Christians are wrong in believing *the text claims* Jesus was God incarnate. For it seems to me quite clear that what the text actually says, using the normal mythological language of the day, is that Jesus' performance made him equal with the Hebrew marginal ideology or as the Jacob text puts it, Jesus made himself equal with God by wrestling with him and prevailing.

These days there is a concerted effort by liberal Biblicists to get around this marginal-versus-conservative choice (and so avoid the uncomfortable marginal ideology which unmasks us all) by arguing that in the Bible God is neither a revolutionary marginal nor a conservative authoritarian figure but rather an indefinable spiritual reality which stands over against us all, relativising all we do and making it clear we can always do better. They don't openly admit this new figure is created by reading the texts through modern liberal spectacles but it must be. For everyone knows the fundamental liberal idea is free competition; the bourgeoisie ideal of a world free of conservative constraints imposed from above or socialist restrictive practices imposed from below. How they manage to convince people this idea of free competition is to be found in the Bible beats me since it is manifestly not there. What is actually in the texts is the revolutionary Hebrew metacosmic[31] god of the marginals, on the one hand, and the conservative revisionists' creation (a religious transcendent metacosmic high god) on the other. What liberals seem to do is stir all of this together to produce an impenetrable soup from which they can then extract, as if by magic, their liberal God. As Robert Browning famously put it:

Ah, but *a man's reach* should *exceed his grasp*, or what's a heaven for?

It's clever, you have to admit, and it gets everyone off the hook by avoiding the excruciating discomfort of what the marginal perspective reveals about our 'civilised' hypocrisy. The only trouble is that it's a complete fabrication for the Bible has nothing, but nothing, to say about free competition and it is disingenuous to pretend it does.

Addendum

Just one last point: how can one explain Peter's embarrassed remark about building bothies for the three celebrities if it is not just a way of lending an air of historical verisimilitude to this oh so unlikely story? Well isn't it true that the text as a whole has this curious dreamlike character simply because it is just a representation: an artificial construct? And isn't it natural therefore that the person who first composed it would register this fact by, for example, writing that the disciples were half asleep ... or that they failed to comprehend what was the score ... or, as here, that they made foolish remarks because they simply did not know what to say?

15

The Miraculous Catch of Fish (John 21)

Resurrection: Vindication of the Marginal Strategy

Since we are dealing with a story from John's Gospel we have to be on our guard. For, though to some extent all of the evangelists colour their reporting of historical events with their own 'resurrection faith'[32], John does so in a very spectacular and pointed manner. This means we find in his Gospel not the tale of an ordinary mortal but rather the story of the Son of God striding around first century Palestine, a situation which, though it may spuriously comfort religiously-minded people, also tends to make it difficult for sceptics like me to take seriously. I am not suggesting that John presents Jesus as a super-human demi-god for it is always clear he believes Jesus was fully human. It's more that he portrays Jesus as carrying about with him a sort of 'divine glow' which would have been decidedly disconcerting had it been true-to-life: which of course it can't have been.

I would like to be quite clear about what I am saying here: it's immaterial whether or not I think the idiosyncratic way in which John paints his portrait of Jesus is good or bad. What matters is that John cannot possibly have wanted people to take what he wrote literally because he couldn't possibly have made it clearer that he was writing symbolically. Let me demonstrate this by considering one example amongst many: John relates that, on being told that Lazarus lay dying, Jesus proceeded to prevaricate for two whole days thus making certain it was only when his dear friend was already dead and stinking in his tomb that he made it to the house to see what he could do! The story explains why this strange behaviour was necessary, for, according to John, Jesus had a point to make … and *that's my point*. In the real world people don't, as a matter of fact, go about making points in such a manner, which shows as clearly as could be that John was writing symbolically and not giving us an historical account of something that actually happened. It also explains why none of the other evangelists have a word to say about this miracle which, had it taken place, would undoubtedly have constituted the medical event of all time.

So we should read this text about the miraculous catch of fish conscious that the evangelist was in the habit of using stories *symbolically* to try and get people to understand the extraordinary nature of this unique historical individual whose life and death, he believed, had politically transformed the world. This being the case we must look closely at the patterns John used in constructing his story because symbolic stories are created by weaving patterns together, the particular way in which these patterns are used providing the desired overall effect. Let me explain:

As I see it John 21 has been composed by welding four patterns together:

1. *A Miraculous Catch*: a group of people struggle over a considerable length of time to achieve some objective (e.g. catch fish) with conspicuous lack of success, whereupon some late-comer inexplicably manages somehow to turn things around:
2. *Peter's Plunge*: an act (e.g. plunging out of a boat) which could equally be construed as folly or daring.
3. *Stressed Nets*: a success which is so great that it puts the venture itself at risk.
4. *The Risen Jesus as Stranger*: recognising the resurrected paradoxically by the fact that he is unrecognisable.

I have to admit that the existence of these patterns would not be terribly noteworthy were it not for the fact that all four of them can be found elsewhere in other gospel stories which themselves include other common patterns not actually found here. For example, in Luke 5:1-11 we find a story which uses both the 'miraculous catch' and 'stressed nets' patterns. Then again, in Matthew 14:22-32, we find the 'Peter's plunge' pattern this time associated with a 'Jesus as ghost' pattern which is like the 'risen Jesus as stranger' pattern though slightly different and so on.

Since the way the evangelists' patterns tie in with John 21 is complicated, I have drawn up a table to give you the overall picture. However, if it makes your head spin don't worry. All I am trying to do is to get you to see two basic things:

1. Unlike real-life events, which are characteristically haphazard, these gospel stories all demonstrate careful patterning.
2. Comparing the Gospels shows that these patterns, once invented, tend to take on a life of their own as each evangelist in turn uses them in different ways and different situations to create his portrait of Jesus.

1. John 21:1-9	Miraculous Catch	peter's Plunge	Stressed Nets (Hold)	Risen Jesus as Stranger			
2. Luke 5:1-11	Miraculous Catch		Stressed Nets (Break)				
3. Mark 6:45-52				Jesus Ghost	Winds Waves & Darkness	Jesus Walks on Water	
4. Matthew 14:22-32		Peter's Plunge		Jesus as Ghost	Winds Waves & Darkness	Jesus Walks on Water	
5. John 5:16-24					Winds Waves & Darkness	Jesus Walks on Water	
6. Luke 24:13				Risen Jesus as Stranger			
7. Luke 24:37				Risen Jesus as Ghost			

(Note: Some people may unnecessarily worry about this pattern business, believing it means these stories about Jesus are simply made up. They are made up of course. All stories are. However, that does not mean that they are *simply* made up. It means rather that they should be read as witnesses to the quite extraordinary political change that Jesus managed to bring about, rather than as verifiable journalistic accounts of exactly what happened.)

OK so you get the general picture. Let's now concentrate on John's account of the miraculous catch of fish: (Row 1). How has John constructed this story and what does it tell us? Well, clearly he has borrowed his basic outline from Luke 5:1-11 (Row 2) To this he has added the 'Peter's plunge' pattern from Matthew 14:22-32 (Row 4) and the 'risen Jesus as stranger' pattern taken from Luke's resurrection story about the two disciples who encounter the risen Lord on their way to Emmaus (Row 6).

Why has he done this? Well, as regards the 'Peter's plunge' pattern you will notice an interesting interplay between the two disciples Peter and John in the resurrection narratives in John's Gospel which is to say this 'miraculous catch' story, and the one in the preceding chapter about 'the empty tomb'. In 'the empty tomb' story, though John arrives first, Peter enters before him. Similarly, in this 'miraculous catch' story though John is the first to recognise the risen Lord, Peter is the one who actually takes the plunge. It would seem, therefore, that John pinched Matthew's 'Peter's plunge' pattern using it here to further emphasise that though John was a leader of the early Church he was not the top man, a position reserved for Peter.

As regards the 'risen Jesus as stranger' pattern, taken from Luke's Emmaus story, it seems to me that John uses this to make it clear that his story is not about a resuscitation, as was the case with Lazarus (John 11) since Lazarus was perfectly recognisable when he was raised from the dead. Consequently, in associating a strangeness and unrecognisability with the risen Lord, John seems to be making a deliberate distinction between *resuscitation* and *resurrection*.

One last thing to notice regarding this pattern business: though John uses the 'strained nets' which forms part of the basic outline he inherited from Luke, he makes a significant change by stating in his story that the nets here don't break:

It was full of large fish, 153, but even with so many the net was not torn. (John 21:11)

I have to admit that before writing this piece I had absolutely no idea what the number 153 here symbolises. What is more I hate it when people *speculate* on such matters since if you allow speculation you can prove almost anything, which indeed is what people regularly do with the Bible. However, Lonnie Woodruff, whose work I found on the web[33], makes a very good case for understanding the number 153 as representing 'completeness on a spiritual, or as I would say, ideological level'[34]. He points out that whereas the number four represents the material, (as for example in the expression the four corners of the earth) the number three, which is often found in scripture, is regularly used in connection with spiritual or, again as I would say, ideological matters. He then goes on to demonstrate that the number 153, which to the casual observer appears entirely arbitrary, has fascinating attributes when examined in terms of its threefoldness. For example, if you take any number under the sun which is divisible by three, then cube each of its digits, then add the results together to get a new number, then repeat the exercise any number of times you will *always* eventually arrive back at the number 153 because when you do the exercise on the number 153 itself you get the same number: 153[35]. Lonnie argues that people living in the first century were used to playing with numbers so they would probably have known of this remarkable characteristic of the number 153. It is quite possible, therefore, that the number 153 was seen by the community for whom John was writing as a representation of spiritual (ideological) completeness. Interestingly Lonnie makes nothing of his hypothesis:

> The number 3 is symbolic of spiritual things. Many of the events in the life of Christ took place in series of 3's. So, when Jesus went fishing, he caught the number of fish (153) which can be found in any third number in the entire numbering system. What an appropriate number of fish to catch. Was this an accident? I seriously doubt it. Am I sure this is why he caught 153 fish? No. But, the number was recorded for some reason and this explanation follows precisely what we know about scripture and use of numbers. I'll let you decide what you think.

Indeed, if you notice, he makes two cardinal errors; first by writing about the story as if it was an actual event and secondly by implying it was Jesus who was fishing! That said, he is surely right to suggest that for John the number 153 must have been significant. So let's see if we, with our god-of-the-marginals appreciation of Jesus' basic outlook, can make good sense of the overall text, using Lonnie's understanding of the number 153.

In order to do this we will first have to find out what the early Church understood by *resurrection*. People tend to think of it wrongly as a Christian word. In fact it seems to have been coined in the inter-testamental period by revolutionary Jews to express their belief that those comrades who had had the misfortune to die before Jewish liberation could be achieved, would someday be *vindicated*. In this way *resurrection*-talk simply became the recognised way of giving voice to a hope that, though at present it appeared revolutionary martyrs were dying in vain, there would come a time when it would clearly be seen that their cause had been just and that their individual efforts had counted[36]. Symbolically they would, as it were, rise on the great day of salvation to share in the resurrection experience[37].

OK, so how can we use all of this in understanding John's 'miraculous catch' story? Well, as I have been at pains to demonstrate throughout this book, Jesus had set himself the task of gathering faithful Israelites so that *together* they could operate as Yahweh's light, the object of the exercise being to shame the Gentile world out of its oppressive and dehumanising ways. However, as we all know, when the moment came everyone deserted, leaving Jesus to perform the task all by himself thus leading inevitably to his death. So what can it mean if John now tells a story of the resurrected Jesus?

Up to this moment in his Gospel John has been following standard practice, using symbolic stories to interpret recent events (the life and death of Jesus) as he sees and understands these from his own revolutionary god-of-the-marginals perspective. However, what we now find is John suddenly introducing what is clearly resurrection-talk. This is a huge problem for, as I have just explained, resurrection-talk was normally used to give voice to a *future* hoped-for-vindication whereas here we find John using it in the interpretation of yet another 'recent event' for clearly this thing John is speaking about using resurrection-terms ... whatever it is ... has already happened! I would strongly suggest this can only mean John was aware of some concrete event which had vindicated Jesus. But what can this concrete event be, given that scholars tell us that, apart from a very dramatic change of attitude amongst Jesus' followers, *nothing happened*. The kingdom did not in point of fact arrive ... or so they say:

> Jesus saw himself as God's last messenger before the establishment of the kingdom. He looked for a new order, created by a mighty act of God. In the new order ... Jesus and his disciples ... would have the leading role. ... We have every reason to think that Jesus had led [the disciples] to expect a

dramatic event which would establish the kingdom. The death and resurrection required them to adjust their expectation. (E.P. Sanders; *Jesus and Judaism* SCM Press, p319-320.)

Scholars amaze me! Because they are fixed to their faces they can't see their own noses. It stands to reason Jesus would have been looking for vindication in the form of *a change of attitude* rather than in a magical imposition of a divine new order *since his whole strategy had specifically been designed to bring about the softening of Gentile hearts.*

But his disciples were not Gentiles, I hear you protest!

Certainly Jesus' followers *thought* they were true Israelites. However, events had disabused them, showing them to be no better than the Gentiles they had sought to impress. This explains what otherwise is inexplicable: that, after the resurrection, Jesus' followers began to wake up to the fact that they could no longer continue to exclude Gentiles by pretending that they were in any way different from them. So it was that the early Christians came to understand *their own quite extraordinary and unforeseen change of heart* as the precious sign that God was at last bringing in his kingdom. They also began to understand that in thus softening their hard hearts God was vindicating Jesus. So they naturally began to speak about what had taken place as resurrection since it was the only way they knew how.

Very well then, having done all the hard preparatory work we should now at last be in a position to read John's story of the miraculous catch. The disciples are back in Galilee fishing together on the lake. They work all night but catch nothing. Not, one supposes, an altogether unusual experience but what does it signify in this story? Given that Mark tells us Jesus spoke of the disciples becoming fishers of men one could suppose that what is being talked of here is the disciples work in gaining converts. However, this is John, not Mark, and in any case the context rules out all talk of mission. The issue here can only be the circumstances which brought about the disciples' astonishing change of heart.

In Luke's Emmaus story, which John clearly has at the back of his mind, the risen Jesus who appears to the downcast disciples as a stranger, asks them what they are discussing whereupon they sadly begin to tell him the terrible news of all that has recently taken place and in which they can find absolutely nothing by way of ideological understanding or hope. Consequently, here in John's story of a similar resurrection event, the fact that the disciples caught nothing must surely signify the same thing: that at that moment, try as they would, the disciples could make absolutely nothing of their situation. They were, to put it bluntly, in a pit of despair. In Luke's 'road to Emmaus' story, if you remember, the stranger Jesus deals with their situation by carefully explaining the profound ideological sense of the events they themselves had just described thereby portraying them in their true light as an amazing victory rather than a defeat:

> He said to them, "How foolish you are, and how slow of heart to believe all that the prophets have spoken! Did not the Christ have to suffer these things and then enter his glory?" And beginning with Moses and all the Prophets, he explained to them what was said in all the Scriptures concerning himself. (Luke 24:25-27)

Once again, given this scenario, the 153 fish in John's story which the stranger Jesus enables the disciples to catch must surely represent the evangelist's way of symbolically saying the same thing. This ties in extraordinarily well with Lonnie Woodruff's contention that, given the mathematical attributes of the number 153, the miraculous catch of fish can only signify that the resurrection was an event that, in softening their hearts, somehow filled the disciples with spiritual completeness. However, once again I have to make it clear that by 'spiritual completeness' I do not mean a sudden blinding revelation of privileged information from on high - for most sensible people an unbelievable occurrence. The word spiritual here must be understood *ideologically* to mean *a sudden opening of the disciples' eyes to the god-of-the-marginals' perspective contained in their own tradition, which Jesus by his life and death had just miraculously and against all expectation fulfilled before their very eyes* (see once again Luke's 'road to Emmaus' story). In this regard the story represents the fact that whereas before the resurrection the disciples showed that they had reached rock bottom (symbolised in the fishing all night for precisely nothing), their unlooked-for but undeniable change of heart (the resurrection, symbolised in the sudden appearance of the stranger Jesus) had resulted in the opening of their eyes to absolutely everything that he had said and done in fulfilling their tradition (symbolised in the catch of 153 fish) so that they now knew and understood everything without even having to rack their brains (symbolised in their nets which, though full, did not break).

Having said that, and having finished this study I feel strangely nonplussed for though John's 'miraculous catch of fish' story tells us a lot about the way in which he was working using patterns and symbolism etc. it adds nothing to Luke's 'road to Emmaus' story which for my money is so much better. The number 153 business is intriguing but that is all. Luke's story gives you so much more atmosphere and, in comparison, John's symbolism seems cold and clinical. On his game John can be wonderfully evocative but here, I can't help feeling, he somehow misses the boat. What do you think?

The Labourers in the Vineyard
(Matthew 20:1-16)

A Parable To Shame All Civilisation Folk

A Parable So Take Care

This is one of Jesus' parables, which means we must be very careful. For, of all the speech forms Jesus used, parable is probably the most misunderstood and the fact that a parable appears to be wonderfully simple and straightforward only increases the danger of people thinking they have understood when in fact they haven't. And don't get me wrong. I'm not going to argue that Jesus' original parables were complicated or tricky, as many scholars these days maintain[38] for they weren't. Since they were designed as eye-openers, parables were originally piercingly obvious, which is not the same thing as saying they were simple. Unfortunately something happened to them, as I will explain in a moment, with the result that the evangelists were left with a very real problem on their hands. This has meant that we too have serious difficulties now in understanding them.

A Parable is Not a Literary Form

However, before we can go into all of that, we must first make certain we understand what a parable is and how it works. A parable is a speech form which means that it is designed to have an immediate impact. Consequently the expectation is not that people will mull over it, as is the case with a literary form[39]. The purpose of a parable is to overcome some difficulty by throwing light on what is causing the problem, thus opening peoples' eyes to what they are at the moment blind. Jesus' parable of the doctor, which we have already studied, is a good example of this. In Jesus' estimation those who criticised him for consorting with the wrong sort of people had a blindness to overcome and his parable was designed to help them understand what they were not seeing in what he was doing.

A Parable is a Complex Illustrative Speech Form

OK, but how do parables actually work? Well, their secret is in offering an easily understood comparison to the issue or difficulty which has now come to light. E.g. it's obvious to everyone that a doctor has to spend time with people who are sick; so by likening his own situation (but not his role) to that of a doctor, Jesus tries to get his critics to see that, in operating as the light to lighten the Gentiles, he likewise is obliged to consort, not with sick people but, rather, with marginals. This, in fact, is the way in which all similes work, for a parable is a member of the simile speech form family. In a simile *a characteristic or collection of characteristics* is highlighted and rendered obvious, as in the following example where the characteristics highlighted are savageness, strength and bravery etc.:

He fought ... like a lion.

In a complex simile it is *a phenomenon* rather than a collection of characteristics that is highlighted, as here where the phenomenon in question is 'thirst':

As a deer desires the water brook ... so longs my soul for you, God.

In a full blown parable (the most complicated speech form in the simile family) what is highlighted is not a phenomenon but rather *an argumentation* along the lines that *if such-and-such a situation pertains then common sense dictates that so-and-so will follow*. In the case of the doctor parable the argumentation is that *if you happen to be a doctor then common sense dictates you will spend time with people who are sick.*

To put it simply: whereas a simile highlights a characteristic or a set of characteristics and a complex-simile highlights a phenomenon, a parable for its part highlights an argumentation. I hope that is now clear.

Illustrations that have Lost their Illustrands

OK, this all seems relatively straightforward so what's the problem with Jesus' parables? Well, it's like this. Take that simile: he fought like a lion. We all know basically what that means because the simile is complete. For on the one hand we have the subject to be illustrated - how he (whoever he was) fought - and on the other we have the illustration itself - like a lion fights. The same thing is true of the deer complex-simile above. However, with Jesus' parables on the whole, this is not the case because what we loosely talk about as 'the parable' is in reality, if the truth be told, only *half of the parable*: the 'likeness' half, to be precise; the 'subject' half (i.e. what is being illustrated) being very often *missing*! This does not happen to be true in the case of the doctor parable above which is perfectly complete. Indeed one has to suppose that it was because it was complete that Mark selected it as the first parable in his Gospel. However, let's look at Mark's first big parable: The Sower. Here's how it begins:

> Again Jesus began to teach by the lake. The crowd that gathered around him was so large that he got into a boat and set in it out on the lake, while all the people were along the shore at the water's edge. He taught them many things by parables, and in his teaching said: 'Listen! A farmer went out to sow his seed. (Mark 4:1-3)

But what is the subject matter this story is supposed to illustrate (or indeed the subject matters of the other three parables Jesus supposedly told people from that boat that day)? The fact is that there isn't one; which is why Mark had to go to such lengths to have Jesus *explain* the parable. Of course, this is a bit of nonsense for a parable that needs to be explained is an absurdity: an illustration that itself needs illustrating!

Stories are Easy to Remember Unlike Actual Incidents

So what's all this about? Well the problem the evangelists faced in dealing with Jesus' parables is not so very difficult to understand. You see, a parable story, as an argumentation, is a carefully patterned and honed affair with not one word more or one word less than is strictly necessary. As a result, however long a parable is, it is extremely easy to remember. This is not true, however, of the actual incidents which the parable stories themselves illustrated, which presumably were things that people had said or done and which demonstrated they were operating blindly in a pig-headed or hypocritical manner. Indeed it is very difficult to remember such incidents and precisely report and record them because, as any journalist will tell you, they consist of a whole collection of seemingly haphazard and un-patterned details:

> First he did this ... then she criticised him by saying ... but then someone interrupted suggesting that ... and then he got up and ...

Because of this, however striking the incidents were for the people present at the time, they quickly faded from peoples' memory and were lost. This meant that years later, while most people were able to accurately recall Jesus' parable stories, no-one was able to remember what particular blindnesses they had exposed. It's as simple as that. So the evangelists faced the embarrassment of this multitude of free-floating stories which they had in their possession but which they could not easily use. In their place we would probably have invented subject matters for the stories to illustrate but, understandably, the evangelists were unwilling to invent things about Jesus.

Strategies for Making Sense of Jesus' Stories

So what were they to do? Well, they managed to make sense of some of Jesus' parables by attaching them to independent incidents that had been remembered for some other reason. For example, it had been remembered that Jesus was often criticised for consorting with the wrong sort of people and so the parable of the doctor could be slotted in there. Some sense could be found for a few more parables by simply prefacing them with the phrase 'The kingdom of God is like ...' A few more still could be given some sense by allegorising them, by which I mean reading some of the component parts of the story symbolically: the master = God, the vineyard = Israel etc. However, the great majority simply had to be left to sink or swim in the general context of Jesus' teaching and in positions in which the evangelist thought they made the best, if ill-defined, sense. However, there were so many parable stories to deal with that the evangelists were unable to include them one-at-a-time in separate incidents or, indeed, in generalised situations, for there were not nearly enough of these preserved in the tradition to go around and, as I have said, they were loath to simply make things up. This means that we now often find them in pairs or even triplets, which is most confusing, for in such a state they not only lose their amazing eye-opening impacts but they also interfere with each other since no two stories illustrate quite the same point. The evangelists must have realised this. However, understandably they thought the most important thing was to share Jesus' stories with others, the business of doing so in a manner that preserved their eye-opening thrusts being, in most cases, sadly beyond them.

Beware the Danger of Seeing the Vineyard-Owner as God

Having all of this in mind, let's now look at Matthew's story of the Labourers in the Vineyard which is one of those 'Kingdom of Heaven is like ...' parables. Obviously this phrase was added by Matthew to let readers know that though the reason why Jesus told this story had been lost they should try and understand it in connection with his general teachings. Since Mark famously made sense of the parable of The Sower by allegorising it, people have got into the habit of making sense of Jesus' stories by allegorising them themselves. In this way they choose to see an important personality in a story, such as a king or, in the case of our story, the owner of a vineyard, as symbolising God (see for example Luke's parable of the prodigal son (Luke 15:11-32) or the parable of the tenants (Mark 12:1-9). This happens now so naturally and spontaneously that people are not even aware what they are doing. Consequently, if you point out to them, as I regularly do, that there's nothing in the text to justify such symbolism, they look at you as if you have lost your head. What they don't see is that reading God into any parable of Jesus, without good warrant, effectively destroys its political sense.

Reading God into a Parable is Usually a Way of Avoiding the Truth

'Why do you say that?' I hear you ask. Well we know for a fact that, generally speaking, parables were used in the ancient world in order to try and cure mental blindnesses of one sort or another and we know specifically that Jesus was intent on getting his fellow Israelites to fulfil their covenant commitment by joining him in operating together as Yahweh's light. So it stands to reason that, in the main, Jesus must have used parables to get his fellow Israelites to open their eyes to what 'behaving as Yahweh's light' entailed[40] in any given instance. And that, as we know, was a political question and not a religious question for it meant loving

God (the god of the marginals) *by loving the neighbour as the self.*
Consequently, reading God into any of Jesus' parables without
strong warrant generally means introducing a new, cosy
religious meaning into the text so as to cover up its own uncomfortable political meaning.

Political Misreadings of the Text

If you don't believe me, just take a look at what happens in the
case of this particular parable. Some Biblical commentators try to
read the owner of the vineyard as God by pretending that what
he did in the story was unimaginable in a human being. They say
that nobody behaves with such generosity towards undeserving
lazy workers who only have themselves to blame if others don't
want to employ them. However, in pursuing such an argument
all they do is demonstrate their political prejudices. For in the
story there is absolutely no indication whatsoever that the
unlucky labourers who were not given work were lazy, just as
there is no indication whatsoever that the owner of the vineyard
was motivated by generosity.

'But that is not true!' I hear you all shout. 'For in our translations of the text the labourers are clearly described as "idly
standing around" and "wasting the day". Furthermore the
owner of the vineyard does indeed describe his actions as
generous. 'So what have you got to say about that?'

Well, what you say may be perfectly true, and this is one of
the problems with Biblical translations. All I can do is point out
that in the Greek text none of this is to be found. Here there is no
criticism whatsoever of the labourers, for all that is said of them
is that they stand about with nothing to do which is what any of
us, lazy or hard-working, would have done in their shoes. As for
the owner of the vineyard, in the Greek text he never mentions
the word generosity. He simply says 'Is your eye evil because I
am good?' as many older translations more accurately state. In
this way he clearly indicates that he has an ideological bone to

pick ... not with the so called idle workers ... but *with their fortunate mates who had been taken on first thing in the morning*. This means that all talk of generosity or laziness in connection with this parable is religious eyewash[41], and a scandalous betrayal of the political point that is being made.

Reading the Text Properly

So how can we read the text in a correct ideological manner? Well, a god-of-the-marginals approach would suggest that the way in which the owner of the vineyard behaves is only 'god-like' in that it is precisely how any Israelite, faithful to the spirit of the Mosaic Law, should behave. Consequently, arguing that, because no-one ever behaves as he did, must indicate that the vineyard owner represents God, is just religious eyewash again. For the truth is that all the vineyard owner does is demonstrate what *loving the neighbour as the self* actually implies and, as we all know, loving the neighbour as the self was what *all faithful Israelites* were supposed to do; whether anyone did it, apart from Jesus, being quite another matter.

'But', I hear you cry again, 'why does the owner describe his own behaviour as 'good' and the behaviour of the fortunate labourers as 'evil'?' Well, it can only be because he believed that the way he behaved *was in accordance with the spirit of the Mosaic Law* whereas the way in which the fortunate labourers behaved *undermined it*. So let's read the story to see if he was right.

The Iniquity of Day-Wage Employment

It takes no particular insight to realise that this story is concerned with the economics of day-wage employment, though you would be forgiven for not instantly realising all that this entails. Day-wage schemes are designed to maximise employers' profits. For when times are hard employers can cut their losses by only taking on each day the number of workers they strictly need. For workers however, a day-wage scheme means no guaranteed employment. This may not matter too much when they are young and fit, for the chances are that they will still find work. However, when a worker becomes old or infirm an economic downturn can mean no employment and since the denarius was a bare subsistence wage this meant starvation for the worker and his family. So, to put it bluntly, a day-wage scheme is a recipe for economic marginalisation. As such, it constituted a huge problem for all true Israelites. However, the Law of Moses was not designed for a perfect world but rather for the imperfect one we live in.

The Vineyard Owner as a Righteous Israelite

So how could 'loving the neighbour' overcome this glaring day-wage imperfection? Well, in this story you find a perfect demonstration of the answer to this question. The vineyard owner goes out in the morning and, as is economically sensible, takes on only the number of workers he strictly needs. However, going out three hours later he finds the marketplace still full of unemployed men. So being a true Israelite, committed to the principle that no-one in Israel should be left to starve, he takes on more workers, expecting other employers to do the same. However, times are truly hard for, going out another three hours later, he still finds quite a number of men unemployed. So he does the same thing again, telling a few more of them to go and find work to do in his vineyard. And so it goes on till, going out again a bare hour before the end of the working day, he still finds one or two men kicking their heels in the marketplace. Scandalised, he asks them what they are doing. At this point, the suspicion must arise in the minds of those listening to the story that the other employers are not doing their bit in making Israel a community in which no-one is allowed to fall out of the net. But the fact that this is all too probably the case does not deflect the vineyard owner from doing what he must and he sends the last few unemployed workers to go and work for him, so that finally the marketplace is empty.

The Coup de Grace

That, of itself, would have constituted a fantastic story ... but, as everyone knows there is more to come. When the time arrives for each man to receive his pay everyone gets the same: a denarius, the bare subsistence wage. Of course, when you hear this you are amazed but the logic is inescapable. In Israel, the effects of an economic downturn cannot be allowed to fall on those in society who are the weakest. So, as a result of his covenant commitment, the vineyard owner finds himself *obliged* to pay the subsistence wage even to the one or two weakest workers employed at the very last moment, the strictness with which he has this rule applied emphasising the ideological importance of the rule itself. Well how about that!

The Socialist Protest

But hold on. The best is yet to come for, unsurprisingly, the youngest and fittest workers who have toiled all day in the vineyard are outraged with the owner. They don't mind what *they see* as his generosity towards their older and weaker workmates. However, if he pays the latter the subsistence wage for working one hour in the cool of the evening then justice itself demands that those taken on earlier be paid a whole lot more for they have been slogging their guts out all day in the heat of the sun. Now, I have to say that as a trade unionist and former shop steward I can see their point. You can't just throw overboard the basic principle that one is paid for the work one does. But that's it. The fact that I sympathise with them only shows that my own socialist viewpoint, which I have struggled all my life as hard as I can to defend, simply doesn't live up to the truth when this is exposed by the light of the Gospel and the Mosaic tradition which it fulfils.

The Socialist Retreat

Though I can easily understand their gripe, when I think about it seriously it's not difficult for me to see that there is something rather selfish in the attitude of the fortunate workers who have worked hard all day. Having said that, isn't it rather steep to speak of their outlook as evil, as the vineyard owner does? Isn't he just selfishly defending his own interests as an employer ... which is inevitably the suspicion in workers' minds? Well, though the suspicion may be there in my head too, for I too have lived all my life as a manual worker, I have to admit that the answer can only be, No. For it is as clear to me as a pikestaff that the logic of the owner's actions is dictated by one thing and one thing alone: a desire to see to it that no-one in Israel is marginalised and left to starve. This being the case, the attitude of these fortunate workers has to be judged as misguided, for if the vineyard owner paid them more, then he would certainly go bankrupt and even more people would starve. This is something that is simply not on the cards. Consequently, in demanding that they be paid more, these workers are effectively demanding that their mates be paid less ... less than the subsistence wage which, once again, means starvation.

Socialism with its Back against a Wall

So I find myself forced into admitting that the attitude of these young and fit workers is woefully misguided. But surely that does not justify the vineyard owner in labelling their outlook as evil? Here I find myself finally with my socialist back against the wall. For if I accept, as I am obliged to, that the vineyard owner has been motivated with but one idea all day, namely to prevent people in Israel from falling out of the net, then anything that gets in the way of this, however much I can sympathise with it, has to be seen as a spanner in the god-of-the-marginals' works. As such it can only be properly described as ideologically evil and horrendous. So, finally, as a socialist, I have to admit complete defeat.

Just one last word: in *attacking my own socialist principles* I would hate it if this was cause for those with either conservative or liberal outlooks to rejoice. For, clearly, their misbegotten ideologies are represented in this story by the day-wage system itself, which constitutes the civilisation problem that has to be solved. As a true Israelite, the parable maker doesn't even bother with such Gentile outlooks in his story for he simply takes it as read that they constitute the evil human world which Israel has been called upon to join with God in changing.

Endnotes

1. The reader should know that I personally do not agree that what goes on in synagogues, churches and mosques across the country today is the same thing as superstition. It may be true that there is superstition present in Judaic, Christian and Islamic practices. However, to properly understand these systems of belief, which are all, to some extent, biblically based it is necessary to look specifically at the Bible. For the Bible has its own take on religion and does not simply reflect religion as found in other ancient Near Eastern cultures.

2. An ideology is the rationalisation of a group perspective. We all think we simply see the world as it actually is. This, however, is an illusion for in actual fact we all see the world in a way that is shaped culturally by group perspectives and so interests.

3. A conservative ideology is the rationalisation of the group perspective of the ruling class elite or 'aristocracy'.

4. See articles by Niels Peter Lemche on the HABIRU, HAPIRU and The Etymology of habiru/hapiru in *The Anchor Bible Dictionary Vol. III* edited by David Noel Freedman, Doubleday 1992

5. I use this much abused word in an ideological rather than religious sense.

6. See http://en.wikipedia.org/wiki/Ex_nihilo

7. For a fuller discussion of this matter please see my work *God of the Marginals*, p161f which you can find on my website here: http://bibleincartoons.co.uk/books/godofthemarginals .pdf#page=168

8. It is a mistake to talk about the Biblical writers employing hierarchical or egalitarian terms because they did not use our top-down, bottom-up way of thinking. They saw

civilised society as centrarchical, not hierarchical, the importance for them being to get as close to the centre as possible, not to struggle towards the top.

9. See http://www.biblegateway.com/verse/en/Genesis%204:13

10. The previous four stories being 1) Abraham in Egypt (dealing with relations with the Egyptians, the ruling empire in place). 2) Abraham and Ishmael (dealing with relations with the wandering Ishmaelite tribes). 3) Abraham and Lot (dealing with relations with the near neighbours of Moab and Ammon). 4) Jacob and Esau (dealing with relations with Israel's brother community the Edomites.

11. Despite say, Exodus 19:24 and 24:2. One should not expect the text to be entirely without ideological contradictions not only because numerous editors, some with revisionist tendencies, have been at work on them but also because no revolutionary movement manages to rid itself entirely of reactionary traits.

12 That is exactly what ancient Israel was; the Kingdom of God. There was no delegation of power to a centralised political system. Mendenhall, *The Tenth Generation: The Origins of the Biblical Tradition*, (London: John Hopkins University Press Ltd. 1973) p. 224

13. See e.g. Deuteronomy 4:32-40 and 7:7. It is possible the Yahwist intended to disclose something about this life-power idea in the name Yahweh is said to attribute to himself - 'I am that I am'. However, I wouldn't want to press the point or give the impression that the above understanding has been developed from this name. Rather, it is the other way round: the understanding comes entirely from the *god-of-the-marginals* idea as this is unpacked when using the partnership principle, a principle dramatically demonstrated in the icon of the burning bush.

14. Not the modern Satan who is the adversary of God but a completely different character who acts as a sort of prose-

cutor in the heavenly council.

15. For more about the Bible's revolutionary tradition and its strategy of shaming see the story of *Tamar and Judah*, Genesis 38)

16. Not taking the conversation between God and Satan too seriously, of course!

17. See wikipedia: The book and its numerous exegeses are attempts to address the problem of evil

18. See Eliphaz' ridiculous list of accusations against Job in Chapter 22:5-9

19. I Corinthians 15:19. Paul was, of course, speaking of a different group of 'Hebrew' revolutionaries.

20. Unsurprisingly we also find echoes of this faithful Israel in the New Testament in the transfiguration (see Study 14).

21. For Isaiah, exile was the punishment inflicted by Yahweh upon Israel because of her refusal to carry out her covenant commitment to operate as the god of the marginals' faithful servant. Naturally therefore, he interpreted Cyrus' decree allowing Israel's exiled leaders to return, as Yahweh's offer of a second chance.

22. See Appendix E in my work *Light Denied: A Challenge to Scholars* which is published on my website at: http://biblein-cartoons.co.uk/books/lightdenied.pdf#page=334

23. See Exodus 3-4

24. See the description of the beginning of the end times in third Isaiah (Isaiah 60:10 and 61:4-7)

25. See Ezekiel's vision of the Temple (Ezekiel 40).

26. By the returning exiles who immediately proceed to build the Temple, much to the disgust of the disciples of Second Isaiah.

27. http://jimmyakin.com/2009/08/five-loaves-and-two-fish.html

28. By and large the same point that the transfiguration story makes, which is no coincidence.

29. It has to be understood that in these stories concerning the faithful servant of Yahweh the contestants are not always the same for very good historical reasons. In the Jacob story, for example, the struggle is between Israel as Yahweh's faithful servant and the surrounding Hebrew communities especially the twin-brother community of Edom. In second Isaiah it is between Israel as the faithful servant and the Gentile world. In Job it is between the post-exilic prophetic group and the opposing group of priestly hierocrats. Consequently it is the underlying political strategic paradigm we are interested in and not the particular historical 'personalities' involved in the struggle.

30. The lip-service we pay to the plight of the marginal.

31. The god who unlike all the other gods in the ancient Near East has no needs which the created order can satisfy.

32. Meaning nothing religious by this but understanding the phrase in Jesus' own down-to-earth manner as indicating that they express what they see, now that they have their eyes wide-open, unhindered by the usual civilisation hypocrisy which affects most of us most of the time.

33. http://www.scripturessay.com/article.php?cat=&id=516

34. The word spiritual is a problem because it can be understood both as a religious and as a political characteristic. Indeed many people play on this and will tell you that the word is useful precisely because it can mean both. However, given my basic conviction that a belief in a supernatural being who can be persuaded to intervene from time to time in human events is a revisionist trait which runs directly counter to the revolutionary biblical tradition, I am obliged to use words which don't confuse ideology and religion. Consequently I can only use the word 'spiritual' if I make it clear which way I am using it.

35. See http://en.wikipedia.org/wiki/153_%28number%29

36. See, for example, Robert W. Funk in *Honest to Jesus* (San

Francisco, Polebridge Press. 1996) pp 274-5

37. Which we saw prefigured in the book of Job when the hero
declares that his day of vindication will come:
'I know that my Redeemer lives,
and that in the end he will stand upon the earth.
And after my skin has been destroyed,
yet in my flesh I will see God;
I myself will see him
with my own eyes—I, and not another.' (Job 19:25-27)

38. I'm referring to the New Hermeneutics movement.

39. The New Hermeneutics make a glaring error in understanding parable as a literary form, the source of all their
problems.

40. I say 'in the main' because, as we know, on one occasion at
least Jesus is reported as using a parable to help a foreigner
see something of what he was doing. See my study on the
Syro-Phoenician Woman story.

41. By this I mean a conservative political point that has
carefully been disguised as religion.

Circle Books

Circle is a symbol of infinity and unity. It's part of a growing list of imprints, including o-books.net and zero-books.net.

Circle Books aims to publish books in Christian spirituality that are fresh, accessible, and stimulating.

Our books are available in all good English language bookstores worldwide. If you can't find the book on the shelves, then ask your bookstore to order it for you, quoting the ISBN and title. Or, you can order online—all major online retail sites carry our titles.

To see our list of titles, please view www.Circle-Books.com, growing by 80 titles per year.

Authors can learn more about our proposal process by going to our website and clicking on Your Company > Submissions.

We define Christian spirituality as the relationship between the self and its sense of the transcendent or sacred, which issues in literary and artistic expression, community, social activism, and practices. A wide range of disciplines within the field of religious studies can be called upon, including history, narrative studies, philosophy, theology, sociology, and psychology. Interfaith in approach, Circle Books fosters creative dialogue with non-Christian traditions.

And tune into MySpiritRadio.com for our book review radio show, hosted by June-Elleni Laine, where you can listen to authors discussing their books.

MySpiritRadio